PHIL TEASDALE

THE BLUE WHALE PLAN

THE LONG-GESTATION, HIGH-STABILITY BUSINESS GROWTH STRATEGY

First published in Great Britain by Practical Inspiration Publishing, 2024

ISBN   9781788603645   (print)
       9781788603669   (epub)
       9781788603652   (mobi)

Want to bulk-buy copies of this book for your team and colleagues? We can customize the content and co-brand *The Blue Whale Plan* to suit your business's needs.

Please email info@practicalinspiration.com for more details.

Thank you

I have so many people to thank with regards to my Blue Whale journey and I am immensely grateful to all of the support I have received with the book.

I wanted to dedicate this book to four people in particular.

Tim Ward, I know you won't be expecting this dedication, however your amazing journey inspired this whole process. Watching your success and dedication to building your business is awe inspiring. Not only that you are just a really nice bloke.

Anne Teasdale, what would I do without you? You put up with my shenanigans, you allow me my mad ideas, you support me, when others would despair. I love you so much, it's a lifetime of memories, support and love.

Phoebe Teasdale, my complicated conundrum, and the cleverest person I know, you have shown me what bravery looks like and it always has a smile. I am so proud of you and love you so much.

Madeleine Teasdale, my biggest fan and my TikTok champion, every day you make me smile, every day you encourage me and show interest and you are the only person in the world that can make me dance with abandon and notice when I have had a shave. I love you so much and absolutely adore you.

Thank you for reading this book, you have no idea what that means to me.

Contents

Foreword

The year is 2013. I am new to the world of self-employment in business. Nervously knocking on the door of a guy I had heard so much about.

Phil was already a seasoned professional, having grown and sold businesses and with a thriving business in play. Those nerves vanished quickly with the welcoming smile and infectious enthusiasm that Phil omits and the line of questioning. I quickly realized that despite his success, Phil was asking me for ideas and suggestions.

Asking me, a complete novice, but to Phil, this was natural; he has a genuine passion for knowledge, ideas and learning. He genuinely loves business, and whether you are on the first day of a new venture or the final days of a long career, Phil is inquisitive and keen to hear your ideas and to give back from his own experiences. The man has not a single ounce of arrogance in his body. A trait which I really admire, and which struck me from that very first day.

Since that first meeting, Phil has acted for many years in many guises in my life as a customer, friend, mentor, sounding board, voice of reason, a source of inspiration, and, when I needed it, a good kick up the bum.

It is said that success doesn't change people, but it amplifies their true personality. Achieving success in his career has further amplified Phil's passion for business, learning, generosity and kindness. To prove this point, after achieving success and selling previous businesses Phil's next move was to set up a business which has helped thousands of companies to grow to a million-plus turnover through structured advice and training. Phil's company has often received significant backing from governments to support businesses and to boost local economies which he has delivered to perfection by building a tribe of followers.

Phil has created an ecosystem for supporting entrepreneurs in growing successful companies, including myself and my businesses. He doesn't offer a *get rich quick* scheme or an online mastermind. He gives you the realities of business and the tools to tackle these obstacles, turning them into opportunities. Covering the genuine fundamentals of business training and one-to-one support for aspiring individuals building a solid foundation for business growth.

Phil isn't just regarded as a leader in business growth by the thousands of businesses he and his company have trained and supported. He is also viewed as a leader in business education by Babson College, which is considered the global leader in business education for entrepreneurs. Phil was recognized as the first UK-based Babson fellow in 2019, working with Babson on developing and delivering business education globally.

A phrase that I remember Phil saying to me is this: "It is not so commonly known that the average time it takes to become an 'overnight success' is around ten years."

Success or achievement in any walk of life or business doesn't come easy or without sacrifice and hardship on many levels. Tony Hawk broke "almost every bone in his body" on his road to becoming the world's most famous skateboarder. Ed Sheeran went from sleeping in a subway station and busking outside Wembley to selling out the stadium night after night ten years later. Kobe Bryant states that he was not the most talented player but adjusting his sleep pattern to train four times a day whilst others trained twice for more than 20 years to get ahead and stay ahead. J.K. Rowling had the most extensive selling book series rejected 12 times. Do I even need to say its name? Opera Winfrey was famously sacked and told she was unfit for television before becoming a globally recognized TV star with multi-billion dollar wealth. The truth is if we want extraordinary results, in many cases, we need to be prepared to do what others aren't prepared to do.

It is also commonly stated that there are no shortcuts in life or business. But I think there are shortcuts. I have learned through my own experiences, through training, mentors and ongoing personal development that you can learn from others. This book is a detailed cheat sheet. It takes a proven methodology and provides practical steps to smooth the business and personal growth journey. I say business and personal, as I feel two are intrinsically linked, as you will realize this as you progress through the book.

What better way to progress than to learn from someone who has been there, done it and got several t-shirts, along with helping thousands of others on that journey. Very little in this world is entirely new or unique; in most cases, you can find someone who has been successful and has built a blueprint. That is precisely what this book does.

Phil's first book, *In Cahoots*, was a smash hit because it gave practical advice to getting going and solving your own personal and business problems, but also for me, it helped to understand what my *why* is to define my version of success.

I continue to strive for my version of success. A version of success that Phil has helped me to understand and to strive for. Finding the most profound and meaningful source of inspiration and motivation aligned with my values.

This book builds on those solid foundations in Phil's first book. This book takes businesses a step further. If you are starting or have been running a business for a while, some serious value and lessons will be learned here.

Not everyone who reads this book will implement the steps. But I am confident that those who do will be able to achieve so much more than they previously thought possible.

Think big, dream big, then times that by a hundred and imagine what you could achieve.

I can't wait to hear the success stories that come off the back of this book in the coming years, and I genuinely hope that you – the reader – are one of those stories.

Tim Ward
Co-Founder and CEO of Opportuni

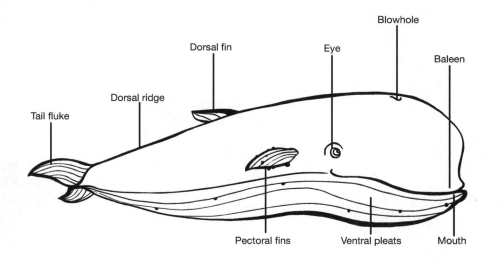

Tail fluke

Dorsal ridge

Dorsal fin

Eye

Blowhole

Baleen

Pectoral fins

Ventral pleats

Mouth

Chapter 1

The definition of a Blue Whale business or a Blue Whale business owner

A Blue Whale business or a Blue Whale business owner is an exceptional type of venture or individual that initially demonstrates a slow and steady growth trajectory, only to experience a sudden and dramatic surge in expansion. This phenomenon can be attributed to changes in personal circumstances, environmental factors, or market dynamics that create an opportune environment for rapid growth.

Akin to the majestic blue whale, these businesses or individuals may remain unassuming for an extended period before undergoing a transformative metamorphosis. This distinguishes them from the widely recognized unicorn businesses (and those of other fantasy animals), which typically experience rapid growth from the outset.

In essence, a Blue Whale business or a Blue Whale business owner or indeed both, represent a more organic and managed approach to business development, embracing adaptability and resilience to seize opportunities when the tides change in their favour.

Why the blue whale?

Here's a fact you might not know about the blue whale, if you know anything at all about them. The blue whale (*Balaenoptera Musculus*) is the largest mammal or even creature to ever have inhabited the Earth. I mean it really is the largest mammal to have inhabited the Earth – ever! Ever!

It literally blows my mind that we live in a time, when due to all sorts of environmental factors we are losing species at a rapid rate – and don't even get me started on the dinosaurs – and yet gliding just below the surface of our Earth's seas, these humongous, beautiful creatures glide along at a weight of about 150 tons and a length of about 30 meters (100 feet). Isn't it amazing?!

I have always been fascinated with whales and dolphins for as long as I can remember. I don't know why, perhaps it's that they are just so beautiful looking or maybe it's their intelligence or perhaps it is a combination of all of these things.

I have lots of whale anecdotes for you and I will certainly be filling you in on them throughout this book, but at this point you must be asking yourself, I thought this was a business book and as lovely as whales are, what the hell do they have to do with business?

Over the last 20 years and more, I have been in the very fortunate position of starting, building and growing my own business and what a journey it has been, but I think I should also tell you, not only have I done that for myself, my actual business is to help others do the same for their businesses.

I sat down recently and went through the last 20 years and came to the conclusion that over that time I must have worked with in excess of 3,000 business owners.

All sorts of businesses, sole trader micro businesses, small- and medium-sized businesses, family businesses and entrepreneurs with two, three or even more businesses themselves.

It's a strange comparison but as passionate and in awe as I am with regards to all sorts of whales, I feel almost exactly the same about those lunatics that take the leap of faith and start, build and grow a business.

So that's what this book is about. It's the description of what a Blue Whale is, why I have identified them as a latent force for business growth in the UK and the world and, most importantly, the tricks, tips, experience and most of all the passion that I hold for these particular businesses.

So, what is a Blue Whale company?

Before I start to tell you, I should in true confessional style, tell you that I run a Blue Whale business. What I didn't realize until I sat down to write this book – or I should say write the 3,254th draft of this book – that I myself am both a Blue Whale and am currently running a Blue Whale company, but I wasn't always that.

I always knew blue whales, I have always been obsessed with them since my early life and yet I didn't know until I was 49 just how they had played a huge part in the development of my business.

It took me working with 15 specific businesses that were at a place in their personal and trading histories for me to develop the Blue Whale concept. It took me two years after that to realize I was myself a Blue Whale running a Blue Whale company.

I have been successful in business, successful not like Elon Musk, but successful in terms of running a business that has steadily grown, has been able to employ and mostly made me a good living and a lovely place to work.

I would like to tell you this came from an altruistic, focussed realization but I am going to tell you the truth. It came from a place of jealously. I'm not proud of that feeling but it was the feeling that motivated me none the less.

I have a friend – I'm going to call him Tim. Tim had been running a business for a number of years. A successful business, one which I had used myself. He had built an amazing reputation and was good at what he did. Not only that, but he is a genuine, supportive, helpful friend and all-around good person.

His business had been running for about five years, had gone through ups and downs, like all businesses. He had employed staff, lost staff, kept hold of things and developed his own groove.

I identified with Tim, I understood his journey, I recognized his journey because I have and had been on a similar journey.

Then during the COVID-19 lockdowns, Tim started to tell me about an idea he and a business partner had. I saw a change in Tim. It was a passion and a focus that I hadn't seen before. Now this is not to say that he hadn't had that before in his previous business, he had, but this was much more visible and visceral.

It was an excitement that I hadn't seen in him before. We spoke regularly during his journey and his passion was contagious. I mean really contiguous. I felt it, but so did others. It was almost as if Tim and his business partner were being propelled by rocket fuel. I was inspired. So were many others. I could see that the contagion that I was feeling was being felt by others. I could see it in the amazing press the new business he was getting, I could see it in the investment that was being thrown at the business and I could see it in the bandwagon jumpers who wanted to be on the train for the ride. I'll admit it, I was jealous.

Why isn't my business like that? Why am I still having the ups and downs, the cashflow issues, the lack of clarity, why isn't my business getting good press? And then I read an article about Tim's business. It described him as the hot new unicorn on the block. Do you know what a unicorn business is? The definition is this:

> Unicorn companies are those that reach a valuation of $1 billion without being listed on the stock market and are the dream of tech companies everywhere.

Now although I was telling the truth about being jealous of all Tim was achieving, he had never stopped being honest about the journey, the highs and the lows. I started to realize something. The term unicorn wasn't just wrong it was absolute bullshit.

The business that Tim runs didn't come from nowhere to this huge behemoth. It got to this place because Tim had past experience of running a business, he had past experience of the ups and downs, he had patience, he had the learning, he had put the time in and most importantly he owned that history.

Tim wasn't a unicorn – Tim is great big bloody Blue Whale.

It was such an important lesson for me and one which I had learned helped me not just become a Blue Whale myself, but it enabled me to identify and work with other business owners that could be Blue Whales as well in brand new ways.

Thinking like a Blue Whale

A Blue Whale business is one which has reached a level of maturity and has perhaps stagnated at a certain level, this can be for a number of months but tends to be measured much more in years.

This doesn't mean that the business is not successful, quite the opposite, it can be very successful in its field and successful financially, it is however stagnating at this level.

A Blue Whale business owner is one who has been at a certain level for a while and is now ready to grow. This doesn't again mean an unsuccessful business owner, but rather one that has reached a certain level of satisfaction – this could be through comfort financially or a place and time in the life of the owner, that means they have also "Gestated" for longer or "Gestated" by design, due to life commitments.

But here is the exciting part of being a Blue Whale business or a Blue Whale business owner, whenever you decide you have met your gestation levels you can swim off to become the biggest ever mammal the world has ever seen.

I recognized that policy and support in the UK – and perhaps the world – had missed these very important businesses, they were not shiny and new, they may not be in the tech industry, they may just be the old faithful businesses gliding along. Importantly it was because of the fact they were just gliding along, moving forwards but slowly that they were completely ignored and often times discounted.

Therein lies the power in these businesses. They, like the blue whale, are there, just below the surface, having both the ability and the agility in changing market places to become the larger businesses of the future, with the right support, focus and most importantly time to nurture their journey.

My Blue Whale journey

I started my business EMS (Enterprise Made Simple) 15 years ago. A business support agency and training company, our job was to help businesses start, grow and sustain.

I love the business. I get to work with the most inspirational businesses and business owners in the world. I get to react to and relate to those that have an immediate ambition to grow, those that are trying to create a steady income and more freedom and those that have an idea that the thing could be good but are a little lost on the journey. We started the business with £1,000 and that was a struggle.

Certainly, in common with every other small business owner I have ever met, we had our ups and downs and everything in between. Sometimes things were very good, other times we had to struggle to pay the bills.

Over the first eight years, we did however build the business to reach around about £1 million turnover and we employed about 14 members of staff.

During that time, I had increased the size of my family by two daughters, one of which had some medical issues and required slightly more care than would have been usual with other children.

My wife was also very committed to her career, which of course I supported, but it does mean sometimes that as a partnership we had a lot of juggling to do, in terms of childcare and flexibility.

From year eight to year 13, we seemed to reach a level of stability that was very nice. Our staff levels and in fact the exact personal stayed in place and seemed very happy. Financially, we were almost at the same level to the pound and because of this I made a steady income. I wasn't making millions in terms of salary, but I was making a comfortable living.

In year 13 things changed dramatically. We had the COVID-19 pandemic and we were able to whether the storm just about financially, in my personal life, my daughters were older and much more self-sufficient and my wife had become very disillusioned with her career.

We had a very frank and honest conversation – she asked me the question "Do you feel fulfilled?". It pulled me up short and before I answered, I asked her the same question and her answer was a resounding "No!". I breathed a sigh of relief and said, "me neither". This set us on a journey of discovery with the same mission in mind, to discover what would make us each more fulfilled.

If I am honest, as I explained at the beginning of this chapter, I was feeling unfulfilled and had been ever since I had watched Tim discover his passion and reignite his ambition for his new venture.

The thing was, and I had felt this in the back of mind for a while, I hadn't lost the passion for the business I was building, but I had very much lost the ambition for both it and myself. The feeling that it could be so much more played more and more on my mind.

My wife on the other hand, had completely lost the passion for her chosen career and even more so it was making her ill. It was not an easy decision for her to make to leave the career she had worked so hard in for the last quarter decade, but it was one that was right. To reach the fulfilment she craved, she would have to step away from this particular career. "How about you?" she asked. "I want to do more" I replied. And that was the truth.

The ambition I once held for both myself and the business was back and it was burning.

It had taken the jealously I felt to ignite it (I am very grateful to Tim for this – he was and still remains the most humble, lovely, hardworking person you will ever meet). Nonetheless, I had needed the push to really recognize what I wanted and needed and what the business wanted and needed.

Through discussion with my wife and my support system, we decided if she gave up her career, this would free us both from the restrictions of having two people working in demanding roles created. It also added a financial pressure to our family.

It was just the forward momentum I needed. A life changing event to propel both me and the business forward.

With a new clarity and enthusiasm, I realized that I had the opportunity to really make the difference, to reach my goals and to fulfil my ambition for myself and my business. This book and this theory is just that. The lessons I and many other Blue Whale businesses and business owners have learned along the way.

Most importantly, I want to share those lessons with you, so that when you feel ready in your life and in your business, you can join our Blue Whale pod. We would love to have you.

Summary

A Blue Whale business or a Blue Whale business Owner refers to a venture or individual that demonstrates a slow, steady growth trajectory before experiencing a sudden and dramatic surge in expansion. This phenomenon can be attributed to personal circumstances, environmental factors or market dynamics that create a favourable environment for rapid growth. Unlike the widely recognized "unicorn" businesses that experience rapid growth from the start, Blue Whale businesses or owners take a more organic and managed approach to development, embracing adaptability and resilience to capitalize on opportunities when conditions change in their favour.

The blue whale, the largest mammal to ever inhabit the Earth, serves as an apt metaphor for these businesses, as they remain unassuming for an extended period before undergoing a transformative metamorphosis. These ventures can be found in various industries worldwide, and their latent growth potential often goes unnoticed or unappreciated.

Blue Whale businesses reach a level of maturity and may stagnate for months or even years before they are ready for substantial growth. This does not mean that they are unsuccessful; on the contrary, they can be quite successful in their field and financially. The Blue Whale business owner typically reaches a certain level of satisfaction, either through financial comfort or life circumstances that necessitate a more prolonged gestation period. However, once they decide they are ready to grow, they have the potential to become some of the largest and most influential businesses the world has ever seen.

These businesses have often been overlooked and underappreciated in terms of policy and support, as they may not be considered "shiny" or "new", nor may they operate in high-growth industries such as technology. However, their ability to glide along, steadily progressing, makes them a powerful force in the business landscape. Like the blue whale, they possess both the ability and the agility to adapt and thrive in changing market conditions, and with the right support, focus and nurturing, they can become the larger businesses of the future.

In summary, Blue Whale businesses and Blue Whale business owners represent ventures and individuals that, after a period of steady growth and possible stagnation, experience a sudden and dramatic expansion due to various factors. They differ from "unicorn" businesses in that they take a more organic and managed approach to growth. These businesses can be found across various industries, and their potential for substantial growth is often overlooked. However, with the right support and nurturing, they can become some of the most successful and influential businesses in the world. By recognizing and embracing the potential of Blue Whale businesses and owners, we can better support their growth and celebrate their achievements in today's global economy.

Baleen

Chapter 2

The baleen

The baleen of the blue whale is a specialized filtering structure made of keratin, the same material that makes up human hair and nails. Baleen plates hang from the upper jaw of the blue whale's mouth and act as a sieve to filter out krill and other small prey from seawater.

The baleen plates are long and narrow, with a frayed edge that creates a net-like structure. When the blue whale feeds, it opens its mouth wide and takes in a huge amount of water and prey. Then, it closes its mouth and uses its tongue to push the water out through the baleen plates. The krill, small fish, and other prey that were caught in the baleen are then swallowed.

The baleen of the blue whale is essential to its survival, as it allows the whale to efficiently filter enormous amounts of prey from the water. Without the baleen, the blue whale would not be able to obtain enough food to sustain its massive body.

So why is this important to your journey to becoming a blue whale? Well, the baleen allows you both personally and professionally to start the process of sorting and sifting through the current business and its opportunities, it's an almost filtration of the data you already have and for you to decide what will be its uses.

Let's start with a practical application

In the first instance, we are going to position both ourselves and our business in an honest way. Like the baleen, we are going to filter out lots of the rubbish we tell ourselves and also the stuff that we listen to that keeps us limited.

By recognizing the reasons why we want to become Blue Whales personally and, in our businesses, we can then do something about it. It's important to be honest with yourself about why now is the time for both you and your business, but you don't need to share that with anyone else. You do need to seek help if you need it, though.

Fear

Do you feel it yet? We are committing to change, committing to changing the status quo, we are moving out of our comfort zones, and they may be comfort zones that we have been swimming in for a very long time. It is ok to admit that this journey is quite scary.

It is obvious that when you start to commit to this journey, you are going to start to worry about the amount of money or time you need to spend or take to become a Blue Whale and whilst you may also be frightened about stepping out of your comfort zone, you will be also thinking about how to maintain that comfort zone, especially if that comfort zone is financially related. How we deal with that fear is the key to becoming a Blue Whale, both personally and in business.

We need to recognize, internalize and overcome it. My first task is for you to think about these three things.

 Task

Write down the answers to these questions and keep those answers somewhere safe.

- In your life, where do you feel uncomfortable at this very moment?
- In your business, where do you feel uncomfortable at the moment?
- How much can you afford to invest financially in this development?
- How much can you afford to lose financially in this development?
- What are the non-negotiables that would make you stop becoming a Blue Whale?

- In that quiet part of your mind, that you don't really acknowledge, that is telling you why you shouldn't be doing this as it won't work anyway, why is it telling you this will fail?

Once you have done this task, fold over the paper and put it somewhere safe, but also somewhere where nobody else will ever read what you have written.

Now – and this is very important – go back and do the task again – and be honest – don't write down what you think people want to hear – write down what you need to hear!

How do you feel about pushing those boundaries a little more? The more you push them, the more you'll feel fear, but do it anyway. The filtration system – the baleen – is starting to work.

People's opinions

As business owners, more so as humans, we always try to surround ourselves with people we respect and whose opinions we value, our pod of Blue Whales if you like. But we try for this not to happen, we also know people who make us doubt ourselves and these people can often be the very people who should love and support us most. I'm going to call them the Killer Whales.

It's hard staying in your pod all of the time. As a Blue Whale you know that krill is the tastiest form of food and yet every now and then you look over at the Killer Whales and those seals they are snacking on, look really juicy.

It's also fun sometimes to swim with those Killer Whales, they do the best tricks and are not so focussed on success all of the time.

But here is the thing, Killer Whales are swimming in their own pod, surrounded by their own sounds and they don't have the same sort of baleen to sift through and taste the beautiful krill.

It's a bad analogy and I know this, and yet the truth of the matter is, it is easy to be swept off course when you are not surrounding yourself with like-minded people, with limiting hopes and ambitions.

It's taken you a while to swim to this part of the ocean, why would you possibly want to change course now you have committed to this forward momentum? Stop trusting people by default, not everyone has your best interest at heart.

The minute you start to claim your place as a Blue Whale, the minute the naysayers will start, the people that tell you to be satisfied with what you have achieved already. Those people that tell you to protect what you have got at all costs, don't look over at the new shiny krill, keep eating the same krill as you have been for the last one, two, ten, 30 years, why would you change now?

These people may be the people that you always thought of as part of your pod, they could even be family members, but once you start this journey, you are moving toward becoming the largest mammal the world has ever seen and also one of the most elusive.

 Task

Make a list of the trusted people that surround you and next to each one write three reasons you trust them as part of your pod. Time yourself writing the three reasons.

Now write three reasons why they shouldn't be part of your pod – why do you have a doubt? Again, time yourself writing these three reasons.

Which did you write faster?

> If you wrote three reasons they should be part of your pod faster than the three reasons they shouldn't, keep them.
>
> If the reasons they shouldn't came faster, consider are they the voices that you want to surround yourself with during this journey?
>
> This is not me telling you to cut dissenting voices from your life but rather, limit the sound.

The blue whale is not only the largest mammal to have ever lived it is also the loudest animal of all. Not only can blue whales emit calls that travel farther than any other voice in the animal kingdom, these giants of the deep also create the loudest vocalizations of any creature on Earth: the call of a blue whale can reach 180 decibels – as loud as a jet plane, a world record.

These are the vocalizations you need hear more than any other – but remember that even the loudest sound in the world can be drowned out by a huge number and collection of quiet voices. The sound a tiny cricket makes, when combined with other tiny crickets is a noise so loud, it can make people deaf. Listen for the whales not the crickets.

What are others doing?

Start to have a look around the ocean to see what other whales are doing but don't spend too long, remember a blue whale is huge, it needs to be always moving forwards.

Now the second part of the baleen process is to consider the data you already have in your business and the things you know yourself. This is a vital tool in our quest to become a Blue Whale and one which we should be replicating on at least a three-monthly basis.

We use data in our businesses currently like baleen to shift and sort and to identify what our customer needs are, when and how they're likely to purchase and to identify any trends we may be able to capitalize on.

If you think about the data, you share every day, to lots of different people, and the data you get into your business, that's a lot of information, we are shifting and we are doing it daily.

It's not about collecting more data, the key to becoming a Blue Whale is more about how to make the most of what we have already.

 Task

Write down all of the data you currently collect in your business.

Make a list of all the different sources and types of information.

Where does it come from?

How do you get it?

Do you do anything with it?

Now, during this sifting process you need to consider:

Are you collecting the right sort of data?

Is it giving you the right amount of answers to give you the information you need to develop your business further?

We categorize data in two ways – quantitative and qualitative.

Quantitative is usually numerical and is great for analytics. It's quantifiable because it's a physical thing, so we can use it to find actual figures. Think of it like social media and the difference between Facebook and Instagram. Instagram is all about the picture; Facebook is all about the information.

Qualitative is all about the picture and explaining the why behind something rather than the functionality. It's engaging but less concrete and so harder to count, and it's often opinion based as well.

If you've ever posted something on Instagram, the comments you receive are in response to the qualitative information you have shared.

Let's consider quantitative data collection techniques

Surveys

When you have a customer base, surveys are a brilliant way of collecting quantitative data. If you ask for opinions, you can also gather qualitative data. They're a way to legitimately approach your customers because you're asking for help, and the information you get from that helps you decide all sort of things.

Lets' say you make jumpers, and you've chosen a new colour you've never used before. You want to do a survey to get opinions on some new styles and shades. You could speak to both new and existing customers and show them pictures of the options.

Collecting data in this way is both a negative and a positive. If you do it too often, people get fed up with answering those questions all the time. But if you do it in the right way and ask for help, people will want to support you. From a response point of view, you can expect about 7%. You might want to run the survey over a longer period.

Data is the conduit to good business because you're able to put in place processes and customer knowledge. You can use a free online tool such as Survey Monkey, and it doesn't cost a lot of money, although it will take time.

Online tracking

This can be done for free using a pixel which tracks an individual around your website. It tracks how long they spend on the site and which pages they look at. It can also tell you if the visitor clicks on a link.

What's particularly powerful about these types of data collection methods is that previously only huge companies could use it. However, small companies can now also use it, and deliver it in a meaningful and powerful way. In the quest to becoming a Blue Whale this is a real tool, that can help develop a fuller picture of new opportunities and information.

Social media

Social media is a great way of gathering data, especially in the early stages of business. It's free, and you can also use it to establish a market base. You can build up a following for a product before you even create it.

You need to approach this from a business perspective, so you don't create the same sort of posts as you would on your personal profile. There are four big social media platforms, and there are tools you can use to look at analytics.

The use of digital media grew at the same rate in the first four months of the pandemic as the previous ten years. The four main platforms are Facebook, Instagram, LinkedIn and Twitter. It's also worth looking at TikTok.

Why would you use it?

Well, Facebook took 16 years to get the 25–55 demographic to adopt the platform; TikTok took two months to get to that. In February 2020, the average age was 12–18, and time spent on the platform was about 40 minutes.

Now, growth is around 97% and it's the largest-growing social media platform. The age demographic has shifted from pre-teen to 60+, and it has the largest amount of advertising spend of any platform.

Subscription and registration data

Let's say you're knitting a new jumper. You have no website and no product in-store for people to see, but you want people to be aware that the jumper will be on sale soon. You might use Google Adverts and social media to get a picture of the jumper in front of more people.

You can then add a short form that people can fill in to find out more about the jumpers. This is subscription, and when the product is ready you can use that data to email potential customers to let them know they can buy.

In-store traffic monitoring

If you're a retailer or hospitality venue, or anywhere that has footfall, you need to work out the best opening hours for your visitors. Here's an example: a family-owned butcher's shop saw a decline in sales when a Lidl grocery store opened on the same street. They couldn't compete on price because they didn't have the same economies of scale. They could compete on quality, but that wasn't enough.

So, they bought a data collection tool from Amazon which tells you the following: who comes into your shop and what time, and how many people walk past. They used it to identify what people were doing and what they were buying.

They saw that they had lots more footfall between the hours of 11am and 2pm than they did 2pm to 5pm or 8am to 11am. They realized that from a productivity point of view, their shop should be open from 10:30am until 2:30pm.

There's a cost to that, because they don't need as many staff, but more importantly there was no drop in sales. Next, the butcher went to see what Lidl were doing. They had a weekly special offer on a cut of meat or theme, such as barbeque.

Because Lidl advertised what was coming up, the butcher was able to offer the same product the week before – they could have their barbeque food on sale during that promotional period. They had a member of staff outside all day, barbequing food.

They also looked at how Lidl kept prices low – this was through not having home deliveries. So, they bought an old-fashioned bicycle with a basket, and surveyed their customers to see if they'd like their meat delivered. Many elderly customers said they'd buy more if this service was available.

Qualitative data

This includes things like videos, audio files, photos, social media, websites and blog posts. You can use these to give you an idea of what your competitors are doing and what's happening in the market.

Clubhouse, which was originally limited to iOS users, grew 500% in three months at the start of 2021. It's an audio-only platform and was the largest growing social media app of the year.

You could have conversations with anyone who was an early adopter at the same time as you, assuming you could get an invitation. Users are rewarded for interactions, and the more they join in with chats, the more invitations they're allowed to offer.

Using a platform like Clubhouse gives you direct contact with potential people who are interested in what you are selling. However, you can't go on and give a sales pitch; you need to share stories and tell people what you've learned through experience.

Tools for qualitative data

These are analytics-based tools, and so many of them are free. Most people are familiar with Google Analytics; Google is one of the biggest data sources in the world their analytics tools are all free. Yahoo is the second most popular search engine out there, and yet most people haven't touched it for years.

You can use a tool to search Instagram for how often hashtags have been used and the top posts. This is useful research into hashtags you might want to use yourself. You can also use this market intelligence to see which other hashtags people are using.

For instance, "#businessgrowth" might be used five million times – if you use that too, the chances are that your posts won't be shown to very many people. Using the data, you can find hashtags that are similar (and appropriate to your business) but aren't being used as much. "#smallbusiness" could be used 14,000 times, so you've got a better chance of being seen using that instead.

Keep researching to identify the top five hashtags that will get you the right types of customers viewing your posts. This organic reach is all entirely free. Hashtags are a way for people to find things they're interested in.

When it comes to the algorithm, it works slightly differently on each platform.

Don't forget, you can also have your own hashtags using your business, product or service names, or other words that are specific or unique to you. Potential customers will be able to find you quickly with your personal hashtags.

Using hashtags (quantitative) along with a picture (qualitative) will give you the results you want, and allow you to build your marketing intelligence. Each platform you use will give you all the data you need.

Artificial intelligence

Artificial intelligence includes: automating your business processes and using data to do so; gaining insights through data analysis via a tool running in the background; engaging your customers and your employees.

Google Trends is a free tool that tracks trends in words, search terms, products and services. It gives you statistics on search volumes on the words people are looking for. Use it to help you find the right language when you're creating targeted, paid adverts.

The UK is still able to access the EU Open Data Portal, which allows us to see census and buyer information across the 26 member states, as well as our own. The UK Government has also set up its own independent portal which holds the meta data on consumer behaviour. The NHS has the Health and Social Care Information Centre, which provides health data sets from across the UK (but not private health care data).

Amazon Web Services also publish a huge amount of free data, including their human genome project. They have a vast collection on all kinds of topics, so it's worth having a look at it.

At the moment, Facebook's default setting is that people wish to be public unless they change their settings to private; new legislation is coming in that will make the reverse the standard. This hasn't come in yet, though, so you might want to look at the Facebook Graph, which takes all the information on every user which isn't private and publish it.

Google Public Data Explorer: this includes trends, finance and other indicators that Google collects. It's all in manageable chunks but can be used for free to build up a picture of your target audience.

Freebase is completely open-access and is a database of people, places and things, and has 45 million entries in the UK. This includes any data you give freely from loyalty cards, credit information and social media data.

For financial data, Financial Data Finder OSU is a great tool. It's a huge catalogue of financial data sets and can be used to filter into demographics such as location. You can get really specific information if you want.

As you can see this sifting process right at the beginning with positioning both yourself with who you surround yourself and, in your business, establishing where you are now are vitally important in your quest to becoming a Blue Whale.

This positioning helps you to make informed decisions and will help you decide your direction of travel with a level of knowledge upon which to build. This whole process gives you the ability to start identifying opportunities: as well as spot the things that are not currently working. By analysing the data, it becomes much simpler to identify patterns and trends that can help.

Often in the gestation period we forget about all of the data we are creating, we become comfortable and because we are comfortable and secure, why would we need to do this.

This applies to us as individuals, only when we start to assess our own happiness by considering the data of our lives can we identify the areas we have lost focus or lost our ambition. Collating this type of data will help us to understand our customers better, including their preferences, behaviours and needs. But importantly it also helps us to understand our own bias towards who our customers are and what their needs are.

We all, after a certain time in business, make assumptions. Often these are made with past historical knowledge, however the whole Blue Whale Plan process depends upon you approaching things with a new eye.

Later in the book we are going to consider this in more detail, but even at this very early stage it is worthwhile considering if you know who your customers are and what data has led you to this conclusion. If you just know, this is the time to reconsider.

Use the data you currently collect to create a much better understanding of this and the makeup of your customer base.

You can undertake this activity once again with the people that surround you, by repeating many of these activities we get the clear waters we need to make more progress forwards.

This understanding can help you tailor your marketing and sales strategies to better serve your customers, increasing customer loyalty and satisfaction, but most importantly at this very early stage, help you build a picture of how you got to this place.

It's time to now start making informed decisions. We want to have made a commitment both personally and professionally to become a Blue Whale, now we have to start the journey using the baleen to get us to that point.

Remember the baleen is right at the tip of the Blue Whale, we have a long way to go, but this sifting process is setting us off in the right direction.

We are using all of this data to provide us with the correct insights that will help us make more informed decisions and get us right to the tail fluke as quickly as possible.

 Task

Using all of the data available to you work out:

- What is your best product or service and why?
- What is your most profitable product or service and why?
- Which product or service should you eliminate and why?
- Which customer group don't you want any more and why?
- Which supplier should you sack and why?

Yours and your businesses core values

Finally, during this sifting process let's consider your businesses core values. Why are core values important to you and your business? Because they're everything you believe in. They're what motivate you, what you feel and unconsciously say to everybody about your business.

The problem is, if you don't take notice of what your core values are, when you try to overcome them by putting a different message out, it doesn't work. As a Blue Whale you should be hyper aware of all the messaging you are putting out into the world so I have an important task for you.

 Task

Find a piece of paper and a pen and write down both your ten core values and your businesses ten core values.

Give yourself some time if you need to, but make sure to write it down and really consider why you have listed these particular things.

If you're really struggling, think about your personal core values:

- What did you want your business to be when you started it?
- What is it that you wanted to be?
- Are there ethics involved, or particular economic or environmental core values you hold?
- What values should your business be promoting?

Once you have your two lists personal and professional, please rank them from one to ten. One is the most important core value and the most important thing that you want people to feel. Ten is important but the least important on the list.

Now look at the list again, and then circle the three non-negotiable values that you want people to know about your business and you as an individual.

These are the things that, no matter what else happens, you'll hold dear to you, this is particularly important during our quest to become a Blue Whale.

It's not about how much you're going to give back to the community or anything else. It's about your individual core values.

Now as part of this sifting and sorting process, I want you to think about your business in its entirety and your marketing messages, and how they align with the values. However you communicate with your customers, look at whether that reflects your non-negotiable core values. If someone saw your messaging, would they understand what you're trying to achieve and what your values are? If nothing else, it gives you a great way to create content to let your customers know what your core values are and why.

You can say to people "use my business, my services, and my core values are…" and you'll find like-minded people. But, if you're trying to portray an image that doesn't reflect your core values, at some point your business strategy will come unstuck.

Remember to sort and sift the information you're putting out and what you want to get from people. Does it reflect the core values of your business, and would you want people to know them?

This is a great start, but it is just that, a very early positioning start to becoming a Blue Whale. Our hard work starts now.

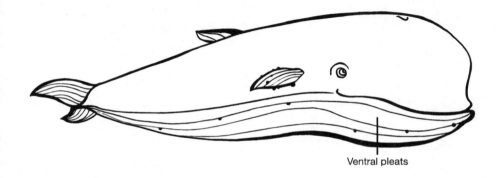

Ventral pleats

Chapter 3

The ventral pleats

The ventral pleats of a blue whale are folds of skin and blubber that run along the underside of the whale's body. These pleats allow the throat area to expand significantly during feeding, as the whale takes in vast amounts of water and food.

When a blue whale feeds, it opens its mouth wide and takes in a huge gulp of water, along with thousands of small krill or other tiny prey. The whale then closes its mouth and uses its tongue to push the water back out through the narrow space between its baleen plates. As the water is forced out, the krill become trapped on the baleen and are then swallowed by the whale.

The ventral pleats play a crucial role in this feeding process. As the whale takes in water and prey, the pleats expand, allowing the throat to stretch and accommodate the large volume of water. When the whale closes its mouth and pushes the water back out, the pleats contract, forcing the water out quickly and efficiently.

Overall, the ventral pleats of a blue whale are an amazing adaptation that allows these massive creatures to consume enormous amounts of food in a single feeding session.

When we think about the Blue Whale Plan and the ventral pleats we are really thinking about how we are going to expand our reach of our business and ourselves and where this development and focus is going to be.

First, we are going to consider you as an individual, and second, as a business owner. Part of the way we are going to become Blue Whales is to increase our confidence both in a personal setting but also a business setting as well.

Not only do we have to gain the confidence to tell ourselves we are going to be Blue Whales we have to have the confidence to both tell and share with the world these facts.

When you make the momentous decision to become a Blue Whale, regardless of how successful you currently are, when we take the decision to expand like the ventral pleats, the confidence and the surety we have had may need a little bit of help.

I know we discussed this in the previous chapter, but it is worth remembering that as we move through this plan we will be undertaking a mindset change and a new focus and approach that can and often does play havoc with our usual way of behaving. Therefore, we are going to consider some tips and techniques which will be very valuable as we begin to expand the reach and the opportunities in our quest.

Whilst we have taken the decision to surround ourselves with other Blue Whales rather the Killer Whale pods, it is really important to consistently practice positive self-talk. We all have that little voice at the back of our head that says: Why are you doing this, you will never succeed, who do you think you are? Try to replace this negative self-talk with positive affirmations.

Focus on your strengths and accomplishments and remind yourself of the times when you have succeeded in the past. There is no one harder on us than ourselves and if you are struggling with this process, find one of those positive people we have surrounded ourselves with and ask them to remind you of the successes they think you have achieved. Hang onto these statements and add more of your own.

 Task

List three strengths you currently have in life and business.

List three accomplishments you have achieved in the last 12 months.

Please write them down on a piece of paper and put them somewhere you can see them every day.

As things change, as you grow, develop and swim to more expansive waters you can change these and replace them with new strengths and accomplishments.

Visualize success

Visualization and manifestation is very important on your journey to becoming a Blue Whale. I know many people, particularly hard-nosed businesspeople balk at the idea of affirmations and visualization, so think of them as business growth tools and suddenly this makes much more sense.

Imagine yourself accomplishing your goals and feeling confident and proud. Visualization can be a powerful tool for building confidence and motivation.

You have to be very careful when becoming a Blue Whale to find that crystal clear expanse of water and create a clear vision of what you are looking to achieve both personally and professionally.

Before you start to create this vision or to manifest what success looks like for you, you need to have a clear vision of what success looks like for you and your business.

Write down your goals and intentions and visualize what it will feel like to achieve them.

 Task

What three goals will you achieve in the next 12 weeks and how will these goals help you on your journey to becoming a Blue Whale?

Now visualize how you will feel when you reach those goals.

Make sure you repeat positive affirmations to yourself so that you can shift your mindset and beliefs to align with your business goals. For example, you might repeat affirmations like: "My business is successful and thriving" or "I am attracting new clients and opportunities every day".

Take some action today, do not sit on this and think well I am visualizing it, so it will happen, visualization isn't just about positive thinking – it's also about taking inspired action towards your goals.

Listen to your intuition and take steps towards your goals that feel aligned and authentic. Remember at all points on this journey to surround yourself with people who support and uplift you, and avoid negative influences that can bring you down.

Most importantly throughout this process, take time and remember to practice gratitude. Focus on what you're grateful for. This is a really powerful tool to help you attract more positive experiences into your business.

 Task

Take time each day to reflect on the things you're grateful for in your business, such as your clients, team members or accomplishments.

Remember, most importantly on this journey to become a Blue Whale, you are at this point and you are reading this book because you decided to take action.

If you are still not feeling confident, sometimes, the best way to build that confidence is simply to take action, just jump in, even if it's wrong, the very action of doing something will set you on the right path. Even if you don't feel confident, take a step forward and do something that scares you a little bit. The more you push yourself out of your comfort zone, the more you will grow and develop your confidence. The more you become that inspirational Blue Whale.

Focus on the present moment, stay in the present moment and focus on the task at hand. Break down all of your big goals and ambitions into smaller, manageable steps, and focus on completing each step one at a time.

Once we feel more confident in our ability to become a Blue Whale it is time to start to really think about expanding the reach and the opportunities for our business. Using the data, we discovered in Chapter 2, we already have a starting point to think about areas we can do more in.

The business life cycle

Let's think about your business's life cycle and its journey to becoming a Blue Whale. Why is the business lifecycle important? Why do you need to identify where you are within that cycle? Think back to your start-up phase – that lasts for about 18 months.

Do you remember the excitement and terror you felt when you started to develop the business? The development of your product and service, the brand and the first sales. It is important to remember this, this feeling, because within your business's life cycle, we are about to become young again.

Remember back to when you had established your product or service and then you had identified your target market, it felt amazing because the hard work was starting to pay off and yet even at this time we still categorized your business as "youthful".

But now we are here, we are in the happy place, we have had growth and now things are comfortable, we know our customers, we know and are happy with our products and services and we let the business really run itself. This could be a fatal place to be for a lot of business owners, because it's easy to want to settle here in the comfort zone.

If you've found a way to increase or maintain sales, you've created a job for yourself. The great thing is I know this is not you, how do I know this is not you, well you are reading this book so it can't be you. In order to become a Blue Whale and develop our lifecycle further, we need to move out of this phase and into the open sea.

This will be a really is exciting period – the business is going well, but we are actively looking at ways to grow. This phase could last anything from three months to three years, or ten years, or 30 years. It doesn't really matter, so long as it's an upward trend. The minute it plateaus, we are going back to being anything other than a Blue Whale. In this phase, we have a choice.

We can continue where we are, or we can look at a second growth phase. You might want to do some research and development to come up with new offerings or find new customers. We can become an even bigger Blue Whale – the biggest the Earth has ever seen.

The alternative is to move into a final stage you've opted to sell your business at a certain point in the business lifecycle.

Have you worked out yet that the theme throughout this Blue Whale process is that you need to know when and where and how, you become the Blue Whale that's just too big for its current ocean.

So how are we going to get there?

Experimentation in this process is going to be vitally important because it helps us test and measure new ways of working and developing. It's not about experimenting in a way that would have a detrimental way on your business, more about finding new and exciting opportunities in a measured way.

Consider three areas when you think about how we will experiment – I think about this as the key to the start of the movement along the body of the Blue Whale.

Is this feasible?

If the COVID-19 pandemic taught us anything, it's the value of being able to innovate in our business and steer it to survival. It's also taught us that small business owners are good at this. But when we are thinking about developing the Blue Whale Plan in our business there are several areas we should be concentrating on in this ventral pleat element.

Although we have spoken about us as individuals becoming Blue Whale, we shouldn't become too hung up in our way being the only way and only our way being the right way.

The key to the success of the plan is to include and develop other people's ideas and input. It would be so easy for us on this journey to suffer from tunnel vision and struggle to know what we want to achieve.

Taking outside ideas can help us to innovate and be the key to the expansion of the current business and its opportunities. It will be very important in keeping focus and often help sense check ideas.

I know that when we embark on this journey, we have to be prepared to accept that some things will fail and not be disheartened or disillusioned. In every business, there are things that we will try that won't work. From an innovation point of view, we need to value this, because it teaches us valuable lessons. We learn what not to do, but it also shows us that with small tweaks we could do things in a better way.

We really need to value collaboration as there are so many other people in the world who are doing similar things to us. The key to this is to use their knowledge to help us to innovate we don't have to think of everything yourself. Because this is the key to growth. It might be with a competitor or someone in the same industry, or in a different sector all together but it is very important to be on the lookout for collaboration opportunities.

We must remember during this phase of the Blue Whale Plan everything we do comes with an element of risk. What it is, is entirely up to you, but you need to know it before you start the innovation process, let's be very clear what level of risk we are happy with, and at what point do we become averse to it.

 **Task**

Ideation

Ideation means coming up with ideas – as many as you can for your business and for the Blue Whale Plan. This is a task that we will come back to time and again.

Every time we feel comfortable or we are back at that place of comfort we will be using ideation techniques to move us into the next uncomfortable phase of the plan.

Ideation techniques can help us move and we will use them for growth, new products or new services development, new communication channels, in fact in every section of the Blue Whale Plan you will be using these techniques time and again.

The easiest way to explain ideation for me is as follows.

I: Identify

We are going to look for potential new ideas for business improvement. We are going to consider what we are doing currently that we could do better?

D: Discover

We are going to use the data we have already developed to find new opportunities. But we are also going to search for some new answers to questions such as:

- What do you need to do to be the best in the marketplace?
- What would make me buy something from my business?
- What is the thing I dream of delivering most – whether I am able to or not at this point?

Look carefully at your business, your customers and your offerings and try to spot the opportunities.

E: Enhance

Looking at my business and the way it is now, how do we explore and develop new areas and new developments to build growth and ideas? What can you add to your business to enhance opportunities? What can you innovate, change or develop?

A: Anticipate

Take the time to identify four sources of change that you can make in your business now to open up new opportunities. Anticipate the future, what will this look like?

T: Target

Which customers are you going to target? How and why will you hone in on them?

E: Evaluate

What are the things that are going well? What are the things that we can take and use elsewhere in our businesses? What is the best thing about my business and why?

Task

A fun task to get you started.

The questions listed lead to a five-minute activity. Answer the questions as quickly as you can, don't think too much about it, go with your gut.

This is a great way to get you started on the journey to ideating throughout your life and your business. All you need is a piece of paper and a pen.

Please remember that this is not all about new ideas; it can be looking at and expanding on existing or old ideas.

When we set out on the Blue Whale journey it has become more and more apparent that we have discovered that 90% of our time should be spent generating ideas and solutions around our current work and 10% of the time should be spent on new ideas or new routes to market.

Types of ideas

For this process and activity, we are going to categorize our areas of ideas into three:

1. Current
2. Dream
3. Implementable

Current ideas

A current idea is something that you can do now or something that you know is possible for you to deliver now without having to change much within your business. It could be an idea which already exists within your business and you can grow.

A dream idea

A dream idea is the fun one. If you had all the budget in the world, no limitations, a team of people to help you and anything you wanted, this is what you'd create. It's your ideal – something you'd love to do and feel passionate about. Remember there are no limits with this section, there is nothing that would prevent you reaching this ambition.

Implementable idea

In between these two ideas is this, the implementable idea. It's halfway between because it's achievable and it's something you want to do, and it's also a new idea or development for your business.

 Task

- What are the current ideas in your business?
- Who are your markets and what are your routes to them?
- What are the products and services you offer every day?

Be honest when you look at your offerings because some things will be working and others won't.

Come up with as many dream ideas as you can.

These are the things you've always dreamed about and think of as flights of fancy.

You've got no budget restrictions and no limitations, so what do you want to achieve?

It's your heart's desire.

Now and perhaps most importantly, what comes in the middle of your current idea and your dream idea?

This is your implementable idea, and something you can add to your new to-do list to take forward next.

Remember this is a quick activity and you will only need to spend five minutes on it, but you could come up with something great.

Make sure you do this exercise quickly and without thinking about it too much.

This is the start of your ideation journey. The point and process of this chapter has been to really look at the ideas and opportunities we have as individuals looking to develop ourselves as Blue Whales and also to examine how we develop new ideas and opportunities in our businesses to move us to this place now the time is right.

Like the ventral pleat on our Blue Whale, we - and our businesses – have the ability and opportunity to expand and develop our reach and our opportunities. What is interesting about this whole process is this. Once we have met the expansion on the first part of the journey, it never goes back to the same shape, the expansion is always there, so the second time we do this, we are already expanding upon the first expansion and to infinity. The larger our amazing Blue Whale gets, the more krill needed to feed him, the larger the ventral pleats get to accommodate the food needed.

The more ideas and implementation we get in our business, the more we expand and build upon the work we have already done.

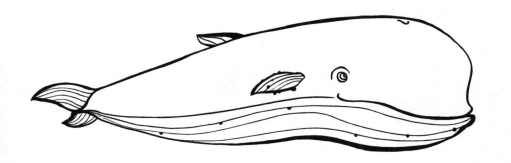

Chapter 4

The gestation

The gestation period of a blue whale is approximately ten to 12 months. During this time, the female blue whale carries her developing foetus inside her uterus, which is located in the lower abdominal region.

Blue whales are the largest animals on Earth and can reach lengths of up to 100 feet and weigh up to 200 tons. Despite their enormous size, female blue whales typically give birth to a single calf, which is relatively small compared to the adult size of the mother.

After giving birth, the female blue whale will nurse and care for her calf for up to seven months, during which time the calf will grow rapidly and develop the necessary skills to survive on its own.

The gestation period of a blue whale is an important part of its life cycle, as it ensures the survival and growth of the next generation of these magnificent creatures.

This is almost the point where we started, isn't it? The long gestation period you have spent getting yourself and your business into the place it needs to be to truly become a Blue Whale.

Although every business is different, most expect to start seeing success after about year four. In fact, the first three years are just about finding your direction and establishing your business as a real company.

There is no strict timeline for success, and we have discussed in detail that the time needs to be right for you to achieve what you need to achieve both personally and professionally, but in terms of becoming a Blue Whale, we are going to assume because you are reading the book, the time is right for you just now.

To give you some examples of how a gestation period can work for many Blue Whale businesses we would normally expect something like this.

First year

Your first year in business will have been most challenging but also the most rewarding and exciting. You put in so many hours of work but you really don't care, you are on this journey and you have to get the business off to a good start and establish as quickly as you can.

Because you are starting from scratch, you have so many targets and things you want to achieve during this period and the even better news is you keep achieving them and setting brand new targets.

Your confidence is at an all-time high, you can do this and indeed you are doing this. You are master of your own destiny and there is nobody or anything that can stop you.

Second and third years

Reality is beginning to set in, during years two and three, there seems so much less to celebrate, just the hard work of maintaining what you have started to build and what you want to achieve.

This is a much more difficult period personally because it seems to be just hard work. There seems much less to celebrate, it is starting to feel like you are on the hamster wheel just to stay in the same place or you are running hard to move forwards.

The best part about this period is that you are starting to really develop a customer base, not only that you are being introduced to new customers in new ways. The website is starting to work and your social media is really raising your profile. It's about this time that you'll really feel the transition from a start-up situation into a small business.

During this time, you will be hiring more employees, be developing new products or services, or you could even be expanding into a new market and looking at new opportunities.

Fourth year onwards

You will start now to see the success you have been working for. You will feel more secure, personally you will now start to feel more comfortable financially and you will have settled into a routine.

You now have a steady flow of new customers, your brand will be well defined, and you'll be regularly releasing or updating your products and services.

Profitability came in around this year and this feels great because seeing profit before you become successful may well provide you with the motivation you need to keep going to reach the successful feeling.

Now what?

And we are back to where we started because you are settled and your business is working well and your life has taken over, your responsibilities, your attachments and your freedom.

From a Blue Whale perspective, even though this has all happened – and it may have taken you 30 years to get to the point of reading this book, the gestation period has still been ongoing.

Until you take the next step, the next jump, the next big splash to become the Blue Whale, the gestation period will continue. It's a nice safe place – being looked after, feeling secure, feeling protected. And yet something is niggling at you. Your ambitious thoughts are taking over your mind when you are resting. You thought you would feel more relaxed and satisfied. You have what you wanted, but life and things around you have changed, now I am ready, I've looked at the data, I've started to ideate and look at expanding the base, but how long is this planning phase going to take and what are the next steps?

Now as a Blue Whale, we are going to take the knowledge we have already gained, our experience and our talent and we are going to reapply it to both ourselves and our business as if we are starting from day one.

Luckily like the Blue Whale striking out from its mother at about seven months, we are striking out from a place of comfort and development and are getting ready to explore the vast clear blue waters.

Our Blue Whale Plan is going to be for us both personally and professionally and although we are going to be mindful of where we may need to be in ten years, our initial plan will be for three years.

Remember when you started the business, by the end of three years you needed to regain your excitement and your commitment, this will be no different.

Thinking about the baleen and the data research we initially looked at, what are the competitive advantages that your business has currently that you identified? We have already developed and ideated the direction of travel and things we want to explore, but now we have to put them into practice.

Clarity in the three-year plan

To get to the place where we want to be, we are going to be really clear and look at several areas within your personal life and within your business to get us to the point that we need to be. Let's position ourselves first.

 Task

At this point we are not thinking about anything form a business point of view. Remember to have a Blue Whale business, you most become a Blue Whale yourself first.

Therefore, putting yourself in the frame, please can you answer honestly the following questions. This will help you to identify where you are in this process. I don't want you to be too hard on yourself, but I do want you to be honest. So, let's start with your feelings towards your business and your business life:

- Is your business meeting the aims or desires of your initial plan, for the moment forget about becoming a Blue Whale and think back to when you started the business?
- Does working in your business leave you feeling fulfilled or do you feel that now is the right time to embark on this journey and if so, why?
- Have you been consistently reaching your business targets or do you even have targets anymore?
- Do you clear your to-do list each day with a level of joy or are you on the hamster wheel going through the motions?
- What does your bank balance look like, is it positive?
- Financially, do you want more and if so, why?
- What does more look like, what is the exact figure and what does satisfaction feel like?
- What does the current network surrounding you look like; do you like it, or do you nurture it because it is helpful in you maintaining where you are and your current level of success?
- Are you surrounded by people who motivate you and those that are striving to be the best they can be as well?
- Have you got someone in your network that will tell you the truth and give you an honest answer? Not just the answer they know you want to hear.
- Personally, where are you in your relationships?
- Do you have strong, supportive relationships around you or is this something that needs to be worked on?
- Are you regularly exercising and eating well?
- Are you in the best physical shape you can be in and if not what would this look like?
- Do you take the time to rest and relax? If you do take the time how and when do you take the time and if you don't, what would the right amount of rest and relaxation look like?

Undeniably, this phase of the process can be particularly challenging, as our internal dialogue often aims to provide us with the responses it believes we desire. Disregard those late-night meals of wine and pizza consumed during extended work hours, as they were simply a quick option to fuel your body during the exhausting 14-hour workdays. Instead, focus on the moments when you made healthier choices, such as having a salad on Saturday. The intention to maintain a nutritious diet is evident, even if time constraints have limited your ability to do so consistently. Therefore, it's fair to state that you possess a genuine desire to eat healthily.

Embarking on the journey to change our habits and lifestyle can be daunting, particularly when we are bombarded with mixed messages from our subconscious. We might feel compelled to gloss over the less-than-ideal choices we've made, as a means of justifying our actions and protecting our self-esteem. Nevertheless, it is crucial to acknowledge these instances without shame or judgement, as they offer valuable opportunities for self-reflection and growth.

In the case of our eating habits, it's vital to recognize that our intentions are only part of the equation. While the intention to consume a balanced diet is a significant first step, we must also be realistic about the challenges we face and the decisions we've made thus far. By dismissing the numerous times we've succumbed to the temptation of fast food or neglected our well-being, we inadvertently create a false narrative that hinders our progress towards healthier living.

One potential solution to this dilemma is to adopt a more compas-sionate and honest approach towards ourselves. This involves acknowledging our less-than-perfect choices without succumbing to self-criticism, and instead, using these experiences as a spring-board for change. For instance, we might decide to prepare a nutritious lunch the night before a long workday, eliminating the need for impromptu pizza feasts. Alternatively, we could seek out healthy meal options within our workplace or nearby, providing us with convenient and wholesome alternatives.

In doing so, we create an environment where our intentions can gradually transform into tangible actions. By accepting that our past choices do not define our future potential, we open the door to a more authentic and sustainable path towards wellness. Rather than masking our shortcomings with well-intentioned lies, we can embrace our humanity and accept that growth is an ongoing process, filled with triumphs and setbacks alike.

Ultimately, it is essential to strike a balance between our aspirations for a healthy lifestyle and the realities of our daily lives. By recognizing the pressures and limitations we face, we can devise more practical strategies to incorporate nutritious meals into our routine. As a result, we may discover that our intentions were not the sole determining factor in our pursuit of health, but rather a vital component of a much larger, more intricate puzzle.

In conclusion, while it's tempting to rationalize our less-than-ideal dietary choices with the belief that our intentions are all that matter, it's crucial to be honest with ourselves and recognize the necessity of action in conjunction with our aspirations. By cultivating self-awareness, empathy and persistence, we can gradually shift our habits and create a more nourishing, balanced life. So, let's not simply say we eat healthily because we intend to, but rather strive to align our intentions with our actions, one mindful decision at a time.

Review all of the answers you have given and make sure this hasn't happened to you.

Clarity in the Blue Whale Plan for the business

As honest as we become with ourselves in the Blue Whale planning process, this also should be mirrored when we are trying to gain clarity in the planning process for this huge step change and movement toward uncomfortableness. There are several areas for us to consider in the process and some specific tasks that we must undertake.

We have started to be honest and think about our personal goals and these are often wrapped up in the business goals we are trying to achieve, but specifically to build a Blue Whale business we must provide clarity on those goals not only for ourselves, but also our teams and also importantly the wider world. Let's start by identifying what we want to achieve with our business.

We are now clear what we want to achieve from a personal point of view within the business, but what specifically are we looking to achieve in the business itself?

Clearly defining your goals will help us to focus on what's important and avoid getting side-tracked, on our mission to becoming Blue Whales. We are going to break our goals down into four specific areas:

1. Estuary
2. Open ocean
3. Deepwater
4. Deadzone

The estuary

The definition is: "An estuary is a partially enclosed, coastal water body where freshwater from rivers and streams mixes with salt water from the ocean. Estuaries, and their surrounding lands, are places of transition from land to sea."

The estuary with regards to the Blue Whale Plan, is based upon your business now, the streams of income and customer and the move toward the much wider ocean.

When we are thinking about the estuary area of the Blue Whale development plan, we are thinking about the economic objectives we have both now but also those objectives to reach our desired outcome.

In terms of specific goals from an estuary perspective we are going to consider several areas. Sustainability and maintaining what we currently have whilst producing an increase in turnover and profitability to reach the desired goal. What is the specific financial goal you are trying to achieve and how does that break down Which areas of growth in the business will affect what you have already?

Let's set some key performance indicators (KPIs) to ensure that you reach these goals once you have set them.

KPI

Key performance indicators (KPIs) are the measurable goals you should be setting in your business to help you hit a particular target or outcome. A lot of people think of KPIs as being income-based only, but that's not all they're used for. Collecting key performance indicators are the key to us having a clearly defined plan to become a Blue Whale.

We must make sure during this process that we link our key performance indicators to our business strategy. We are not looking to come up with random KPIs that don't link to anything, what's the point? We must align them to our strategic goals and our new Blue Whale Plan.

All of the KPI's or goals we are setting during this process must be measurable, we need to be able to check and make sure that the goals to achieve our ambition are provable and outcome driven.

Importantly we are going to update our goals or KPI's at least every six months to continue to stretch and challenge our business.

Open ocean

The open ocean also known as the pelagic zone, is the area of the ocean outside of coastal areas. Here you will find some of the biggest marine life species. Species here are affected by wave and wind activity, pressure, water temperature and prey.

When we look to set some specific goals in this area, we are considering the marine life we will be finding. From a Blue Whale Plan perspective marine life is the definition we are giving our customers and employees.

Goals around this area may well include:

- Goals around the development of the current customer base: are we going to need to add to it or are we going to need to concentrate on value as a growth tool?
- Staff members: do we need to upskill to reach the levels we are setting the goals to reach or are we going to have to add additional skills to the team and its development?
- Competitors: are we moving into a market that is currently monopolized by a competitor, how will we take them on, or specifically what goal constitutes a win here?
- Sales channels: are we going to need to develop new sales channels? If so, which? What measurable outcome would be considered success and why?

Deepwater

The deepwater of the sea is broadly defined as the ocean depth where light begins to fade, at an approximate depth of 200 metres (656 feet) or the point of transition from continental shelves to continental slopes. Conditions within the deepwater are a combination of low temperatures, darkness and high pressure. The deepwater is considered the least explored Earth biome, with the extreme conditions making the environment difficult to access and explore.

From a goal perspective the deepwater is perhaps the hardest to explain. Up until this point the goals we have set are similar to the goals any business would set to look at a growth cycle.

From a Blue Whale perspective, the deepwater goals are the most difficult to navigate, because they are the underpinning goals that perhaps don't get the visible attention but are the most important to actually succeeding in becoming a Blue Whale business.

These goals are really the sacrifices you are willing to make to achieve the ambition. It could be things such as family time, travelling or even initial monetary reward to achieve the Blue Whale outcome.

The goals you might consider in this element will be the non-negotiables and perhaps those you will only share with a select few. These areas could be things such as relationships, health, standard of living, your reputation, stability and your pride, all discussed below.

Relationships

The goal here may be to ensure that you maintain some important relationships, however, as an evolving Blue Whale you must be ready to sacrifice some relationships because it is going to happen.

You have to cut off a few relationships in order to grow. The goal here is to jettison the right relationships for the right reasons.

Health

In order to succeed in life, you should be healthy first, rather than wealthy. You must set some specific health goals for both yourself and your team. It is easy to fall into the trap of working to burnout and to foster a similar culture, your goal here should be to create a culture that rewards good health and self-care.

Standard of living

You may need to take a hit to your current standard of living to hit your goal, so specifically what is the absolute bottom line, set a target or goal and don't go past it. In order to make a higher standard of living you have to be consistent about your goal. You may have to downsize, there may be no holidays and no meals out for a while whilst you start on this journey.

Your reputation

Remember when you're on your path to success people will be quick to point out the things you are getting wrong and the risks you are taking. Remember change is hard. You have chosen this path but the others in your business and in your personal life have not.

Set some specific goals, to talk about why you are doing this, what you are hoping to achieve and impart this information regularly.

Stability

We got to this point because we were feeling stable and somewhat stuck and whilst stability was the thing that has motivated us to strike out, it is also the thing that holds us back.

Think specifically about a goal that incorporates a minimum level of stability for you and what this will look like.

Your pride

To become a Blue Whale, you may need to sacrifice your perceived standing in the circles you currently travel. The goal here is to surround yourself with people to look up to, rather than people that look up to you. Your goal is to identify at least four of these people to help you form a useful network.

No matter what kind of success you are trying to pursue, you must let go of your pride in order to move forward in your success journey.

If you are unwilling to accept your mistakes and failures, you will never learn and improve and become a Blue Whale. It is when you put down your pride and accept what is working, only then will you be able to succeed on this journey.

The deadzone

Deadzones are low-oxygen, or hypoxic, areas in the world's oceans and lakes. Because most organisms need oxygen to live, few organisms can survive in hypoxic conditions. That is why these areas are called deadzones.

On your journey to becoming a Blue Whale we are going to consign a number of people, contacts, friends and acquaintances to the deadzone.

This sounds worse than it is, we are simply going to concentrate on those groups of people that help us reach our goals. Our target here is to identify those that we have to consign to the zone and justify why we have done it.

The goal in the ocean was to expand our list of people, here the goal is to limit the group to those that make the biggest impact.

When you're thinking about the strategic partnerships that you would like to build, there are a couple of things to consider. Remember, it's a partnership; they're not taking over your business. You'll bring something to it and they'll bring their resources.

Think about the strategic partnerships that will help you. They can often help increase the technology you use in your business, for example, which can be invaluable. If you want to enter new markets, a strategic partnership will help you to do that. But the goal here is to consider and make sure you have clearly identified those partnerships and that you have jettisoned the rest.

Now set a goal to get rid of some clients or customers, send them off into the deadzone. Here's why:

- There are a number of reasons you might want to fire a client, and if you feel like it's something you need to do, that's often a sign that something's gone wrong in the relationship.
- Is the profit margin non-existent? Have you fallen into a trap where you have a number of clients but you're not making a

profit? But you service them anyway because they are loyal customers.

- Let's be honest – do you just not like them? Clear them out – we are making the path to becoming a Blue Whale, we don't want any more hurdles.

Set some specific goals and measurable numbers.

Throughout the gestation period and beyond we have really been planning to move out into the open water. With good planning and goal setting, personally and professionally this journey will move much more swiftly and with a clear purpose and focussed outcome.

Take the time to start to not just verbalize this plan, but also to commit it to paper, the process to becoming a Blue Whale is going to need constant review and checking, but most of all it will require these clear goals and clearly defined outcomes.

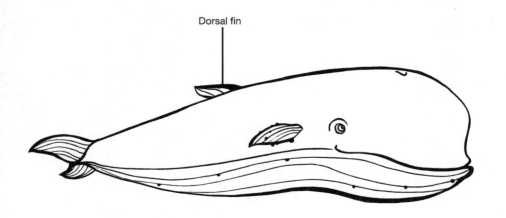

Dorsal fin

Chapter 5

The dorsal fin

The blue whale has a dorsal fin located near the centre of its back. However, unlike the dorsal fins of many other whale species, the dorsal fin of a blue whale is relatively small and triangular in shape, measuring only about 1–2 feet (30–60 cm) in height.

The small size of the dorsal fin is thought to be an adaptation to the blue whale's massive size and streamlined body shape, which enables it to swim efficiently through the water without the need for a large fin to provide stability or manoeuvrability. Additionally, the small dorsal fin may help reduce drag and allow the whale to swim faster and more efficiently.

It's important to note that not all blue whales have a dorsal fin, as some individuals have a completely smooth back. The reason for this variation is not fully understood, but it may be due to genetics or environmental factors.

From the perspective of the Blue Whale Plan when we think about the dorsal fin, we are really thinking about the thing that will break the water first, and the fact that as a small section of the way, it is essential to providing balance and ballast.

Developing a Blue Whale Plan for yourself and your business is fine if you live in a complete silo and do not have any customers or staff members, however, at this point you wouldn't be looking to develop yourself and your business into Blue Whales if this was the case.

Therefore, to achieve this ballast, to get people inside and outside of your business to really buy into the concepts of what you are trying to achieve we really must consider a number of factors.

Internally within an organization

So, as we are about to go through a period of growth and change in our businesses, we may have a struggle to get your existing staff on board, to get them to recognize why we are going through this change and most importantly buy into the change and not work against it.

First and foremost, it's important to understand that change can be scary for some people. They may feel unsure of how their job will be impacted or worry about what the future holds.

Communication is the absolute key to overcoming this, and in the instance of this rapid growth and development, honest and effective communication hold the key.

When developing ourselves and our business we need to be totally transparent and open about what's happening in the business, why it's happening and how it will impact everyone.

It is absolutely fine to create a dialogue and encourage our staff to ask questions and voice their concerns. To get buy-in and for our staff and employees to understand the journey we are on we need to help them to feel heard and included in the process.

 Task

To improve communication and to start the process of the Blue Whale Plan, we are going to start the process of opening clear communication channels with our employees based around a process called dialogic talk.

The key to this process is making sure that everyone is heard, everyone can contribute and most of all, participants feel valued and supported.

Collect staff members together in groups of no more than six participants and explain that you are undertaking a plan to grow and develop the business and yourself and most importantly explain as fully as you can or you want to share, why you are doing this.

The purpose of this is to be a reciprocal form of listening, sharing and considering the view of others, therefore let everyone have a turn to speak and offer this in a supportive way so that all participants will be able to express themselves clearly and safely.

The key to this process is twofold, as the discussions progress, we then need to build on their and others' contributions and our role as a Blue Whale is to channel them into as a group, a coherent line of thinking.

The purpose of the whole task is to make the participants feel valued, engaged, listen to and most importantly part of the Blue Whale Plan journey. Like the dorsal fin, it doesn't matter how big the group or fin is, the most important part is that it helps to move things forward in a stable and secure manner.

Another strategy to consider is involving your staff in the decision-making process. You may not be able to involve everyone in every decision, but finding opportunities to seek input and feedback can go a long way in getting buy-in. This can include things like soliciting ideas for how to handle a particular challenge or getting input on the implementation of a new process.

By involving your staff in the decision-making process, you're not only getting their buy-in, but you're also empowering them to take ownership of the changes happening in the business.

Communication in this whole process is the key

It is very important to recognize that different people have different communication styles. Some people may prefer to have one-on-one conversations, while others may be more comfortable in group settings.

Make sure to communicate in a way that works for your staff. This may mean having regular team meetings, setting up one-on-one check-ins or providing written updates. Whatever approach you take, make sure it's tailored to the needs and preferences of your staff.

When it comes to change, it's also important to be patient and this is a very difficult part of the Blue Whale Plan. You made the decision to follow this process, you came to this process with a desire to grow personally and professionally and you wanted to move out of the feeling of stagnation that you felt. However, people in your organization may need time to process and adjust to the new normal. Don't expect everyone to be on board immediately. Instead, be patient and provide ongoing support and encouragement.

Celebrate small wins and acknowledge progress along the way. This will help your staff see that the changes are making a positive impact and will motivate them to continue moving forward.

Training and development

Like you are trying something new to build your experience, to explore other opportunities and trying to develop yourself and your business, another strategy to consider for your staff is to provide training and development opportunities.

As your business grows and changes, your staff will need to develop new skills and knowledge to keep up. By providing training and development opportunities, you're not only helping your staff grow and develop, but you're also showing that you're invested in their success. This can help foster a sense of loyalty and commitment, which can translate into greater buy-in for the changes happening in the business, you may also spot a number of Blue Whale calves along the way that will really help you develop and build your pod much faster.

Finally, it's important to lead by example. As a leader, your attitude and behaviour can have a significant impact on your staff. If you're excited and passionate about the changes happening in the business, your staff will be more likely to get on board. Conversely, if you're negative or resistant to change, your staff may be hesitant to embrace it. Make sure you're modelling the behaviours and attitudes you want to see from your staff.

Getting this vitally important buy-in from your existing staff during a period of growth and change requires effective communication, involvement in the decision-making process, patience, training and development, and leading by example.

By taking a friendly and supportive approach you can help your staff navigate the transition and feel empowered to take ownership of the changes happening in the business.

Remember, change can be scary, it feels that way for you as well after a period of stability and stasis but with the right strategies and support, you and your staff can successfully navigate this new chapter in your business's journey.

One word of warning

The Blue Whale Plan embraces change and a renouncement of the status quo and this can be too much for some people. You will lose some people on this journey and these people may have been with you for a long time, may have been instrumental in the initial growth of your business.

You must be prepared for this and whilst it will make you sad, remembering the previous chapter, this is part of the process and will happen as the ocean becomes a much wider place to swim.

Externally outside of your organization

We have identified that putting the Blue Whale Plan into practice inside an organization can and will be very challenging, it will be even more so if you are unable to bring your current and new external contacts to buy into the process.

Implementing the plan and moving away from the status quo is always going to be a very challenging thing to do and one of the most important things to we need to do to help this process to successfully navigate this growth and change is getting buy-in from external stakeholders.

Stakeholders

Who are your external stakeholders?

When you think about who your external stakeholders may be there are a number of people you may want to consider. These stakeholders may include customers, suppliers, investors, regulatory bodies and other third parties.

When thinking about who your stakeholders may be and why we want them on board as part of the Blue Whale Plan, it may be easier to subcategorize them in the following ways.

Primary stakeholders

These are the people with whom you will be directly affecting them, either positively or negatively, when you start to implement change and move from the stasis you have found yourself in, to the fast-paced development phase on which you are now embarking.

Secondary stakeholders

These are the people that are indirectly affected, either positively or negatively, by the changes you are making. These may be people considering your service but not a direct customer, those that have bought from you in the past but no longer do so, suppliers into the business on an intermittent basis etc.

Key stakeholders

Finally, and perhaps most importantly, these are the stakeholders who might belong to either or neither of the first two groups, but are those who can have a positive or negative effect on an effort, or who are important to an organization.

Examples of key stakeholders might be funders, government officials, head of businesses, community figures or any other person that would wield a significant amount of influence and have a direct impact on the decisions you are making.

 Task

Get together with people in your organization, involved in or informed about the effort you are introducing for either yourself or your business to become a Blue Whale and start calling out categories and names.

Things such as postal services, stationary suppliers, caterers or even things such as childcare support.

Shout out anything that comes to mind, even if it seems silly. On reflection, the silly ideas can turn out to be among the best, so be as far-ranging as you can.

After ten or 15 minutes, stop and discuss each suggestion, perhaps identifying each as a primary, secondary and/or key stakeholder.

Make a list and then start to build relationships.

Building relationships with external stakeholders

The first step in getting buy-in from external stakeholders is to communicate openly and honestly. When a company is going through growth and change, there may be a tendency to keep things under wraps until everything is set in stone. However, this approach can be counterproductive.

Stakeholders are more likely to be supportive if they feel that they are part of the process from the beginning. This means communicating early and often about the company's plans and the rationale behind them. Open and honest communication also means being transparent about the risks and challenges associated with the growth and change.

Stakeholders will be more likely to support the whole process if they understand the potential pitfalls and are confident that the company has a plan to mitigate them. This requires a willingness to be vulnerable and acknowledge that not everything will go according to plan. Throughout the whole Blue Whale process, we are asking you to expose your vulnerability and act and acknowledge both the positive and negative parts of your journey.

Involve your stakeholders in the process

Another strategy for getting buy-in from external stakeholders is to involve them in the process. This means soliciting feedback and input from stakeholders and incorporating it into the company's plans. For example, if the company is planning to expand its product line, it could survey its customers to find out which products they would be most interested in. If the company is planning to implement new technology, it could consult with its suppliers to ensure that the new technology is compatible with their systems.

Involving stakeholders in the process also means addressing their concerns and objections, do not shy away from acknowledging the negatives as well as the positive outcomes you are pursuing.

Build partnerships

Another strategy for getting buy-in from external stakeholders is to build relationships based on trust and mutual benefit. This means treating stakeholders as partners rather than adversaries. For example, the company could offer incentives to suppliers who are willing to work with it to implement new processes or technologies. The company could also offer discounts or other benefits to customers who are willing to provide feedback on new products or services.

Building relationships based on trust and mutual benefit requires a long-term perspective. It means investing in relationships even when there is no immediate benefit to the company. For example, the company could sponsor community events or donate to local charities to demonstrate its commitment to the community.

It is important to recognize that getting buy-in from external stakeholders is not a one-time event. It requires ongoing communication and engagement. This means providing regular updates on the company's progress and being responsive to feedback and concerns. It also means recognizing and celebrating the contributions of external stakeholders to the company's success.

To make a success of the Blue Whale Plan and to build the momentum required getting buy-in from external stakeholders is critical to the success of a company that is going through this growth and change. This requires open and honest communication, involvement of stakeholders in the process, building relationships based on trust and mutual benefit and ongoing engagement.

It is important that for you as a Blue Whale that you follow these strategies, a true Blue Whale will build a supportive network of stakeholders who will help them navigate the challenges of growth and change.

Stability

It seems counter intuitive when from the start of the Blue Whale Plan, we have been asking to move out of our comfort zone, away from the stable and somewhat predictable place we have found ourselves in, to then start to talk about stability. However, to become a Blue Whale business, there must be some element of stability from which to grow.

We all know that running a business of whatever size is a challenging task. It involves managing a variety of moving parts, including finances, personnel and resources. However, when we start to talk about growth and development, one key factor that is often overlooked is stability.

Stability is essential for business growth, and it can be the difference between a thriving business but secure business and a thriving growth business.

Stability refers to the ability of a business to maintain a consistent level of performance over time. This means that the business is able to generate steady revenue, manage its expenses effectively, and maintain a strong customer base. Stability is essential for business growth because it provides a solid foundation on which the business can build and expand.

There are several reasons why I say stability is essential for business growth. First, stability provides a sense of security and predictability – the very reason we are looking to become Blue Whales. When a business is stable, employees and customers know what to expect. This creates a sense of trust and confidence that can be invaluable in the competitive world whilst we are trying to develop the business and the Plan much further.

Customers are more likely to return to a business that they trust, and employees are more likely to stay with a business that provides them with a stable and predictable work environment, this does not mean an environment without new ideas, area of excitement and constant innovation.

Second, stability enables a business to invest in its future. When a business is stable, it has the financial resources and flexibility to invest in new products, services or markets. This can help the business to expand and diversify its offerings, which in turn can help to attract new customers and generate more revenue.

However, if a business is constantly struggling to make ends meet it will not have the resources or the confidence to take these kinds of risks, so some financial stability is the key to the success of the Blue Whale Plan. A business without financial stability can still become a Blue Whale business, but it will be a slightly harder journey.

Third, stability can help a business to weather economic downturns or other unexpected events. No business is immune to economic turbulence, and there will always be unexpected challenges that arise. However, a stable business is better equipped to handle these challenges than one that is struggling to survive.

A stable business will have reserves of cash and other resources that it can draw on during difficult times. It will also be better able to adapt to changing market conditions or customer preferences. If you are not at this place yet either personally or professionally, please don't despair.

There are several key factors that contribute to a stable business and you can start to work on these with immediate effect. The overall contribution to your business becoming a Blue Whale will be massively enhanced by it.

Financial management

A business that is stable must be able to manage its finances effectively. This means creating a budget, tracking expenses and revenue, and making smart investments in the future. It also means being disciplined about controlling costs and avoiding unnecessary expenditures.

Customer satisfaction

A stable business must be able to attract and retain customers. This requires providing high-quality products or services, delivering excellent customer service, and building strong relationships with customers. A business that is able to consistently meet the needs of its customers will be more likely to maintain a stable customer base.

Employee satisfaction

Having satisfied employees is also an important factor in achieving stability. A business that is able to create a positive work environment, provide competitive compensation and benefits, and offer opportunities for growth and development will be more likely to retain its employees. This, in turn, can help to maintain stability by reducing turnover and creating a more cohesive and effective team.

Adaptation

Finally, a business must be able to adapt to changing conditions. This means being flexible and responsive to new opportunities and challenges. A business that is too rigid or set in its ways may struggle to adapt to changing market conditions or customer preferences.

However, a business that is open to new ideas, willing to take risks, and able to learn from its mistakes will be better positioned to achieve stability and grow over time.

These areas together form the dorsal fin of the Blue Whale Plan, internal and external stakeholder development and buy in, developed from a stable base. The Blue Whale Plan for your business is starting to come together and your confidence and movement towards this process should now be starting to build.

From my own perspective as I moved through this process, this was the point that I truly realized I was now on a journey that would be difficult to stop. I was feeling more focussed, more in charge and most importantly much more in control both personally and professionally.

 Weekly task

How do you feel at this point?

Write down the three things you feel about yourself and your business at this moment.

Dorsal ridge

Chapter 6

The dorsal ridge

The dorsal ridge of a blue whale refers to a raised structure that runs along the top of the whale's body from the blowhole to the tail flukes.

The dorsal ridge of a blue whale is an important physical characteristic that helps scientists identify individuals and track their movements. The shape and size of the dorsal ridge can vary slightly among individuals, making it possible to distinguish one whale from another.

In addition to aiding in identification, the dorsal ridge also plays a role in the whale's movement through the water. It helps to reduce drag and stabilize the whale's body as it swims, allowing for efficient movement through the water.

Just as the dorsal ridge is an essential part of the tracking system of the blue whale, tracking all elements during this rapid growth period in a business is essential.

Tracking involves monitoring and measuring various aspects of the business, such as finances, sales, stock and customer satisfaction, to ensure that it is performing at its best. Tracking helps us during this period to make informed decisions, identify areas for improvement and stay competitive in our industries.

This is a critical task for us because it provides even more valuable insights into the performance of the business. It helps us make informed decisions based on accurate data, rather than relying on assumptions or guesswork. Tracking also allows us to identify areas for improvement and make adjustments to our operations to optimize our performance.

Strategic financial management

We always need to track our income, expenses and cashflow to ensure they are profitable and sustainable, but during this period of growth, we need to do this even more so. Accurate financial tracking can us identify areas where we can reduce costs, increase revenue or improve cashflow. It can also help us make informed decisions about investments, loans and other financial matters.

Strategic financial management is essential for this part of the Blue Whale Plan where we are strategically and rapidly growing the business. It is vitally important to note that a business can only achieve its goals if it has the right financial resources, planning and management.

Strategic financial management is a process that involves planning, organizing, controlling and directing the financial resources of an organization to achieve its objectives.

One of the most important reasons for implementing strategic financial management is to ensure that a business has the necessary financial resources to grow. A business that has a well-planned financial strategy will be able to allocate resources efficiently and effectively. This will give you the ability during this rapid growth period to be able to invest in the areas that have the potential to generate the most return on investment (ROI). For example, a business that has identified a new market or product line that has significant growth potential can allocate financial resources to that area to maximize its growth potential.

 Task

Identify three areas in your plan for rapid growth that will require some sort of investment. Be specific, work out what the exact costs will be. Where will the money come from to make this investment?

What return on investment (ROI) specifically would you require for this investment to be a success?

Risk

Strategic financial management also helps a business to manage risks. Every business face risks, such as market risk, credit risk and operational risk.

By implementing a sound financial management strategy, a business can identify and manage these risks effectively. This means that the business will be better able to respond to unforeseen events that could negatively impact its growth.

 Task

Identify the areas in your business that would present a risk to your business – as it is now and as it would be once you have made the investment in the areas we have just identified.

Cashflow

Another major benefit during this rapid growth phase of the Blue Whale Plan with regards to strategic financial management is that it will help you to optimize your cashflow.

Cashflow is the lifeblood of any business, and managing it effectively is critical for long-term success. By implementing a sound financial management strategy, a business can optimize its cashflow by managing its accounts receivable and accounts payable effectively, improving its working capital management, and forecasting its cashflow accurately.

Task

Put together a cashflow forecast for your business, examining three scenarios.

Scenario 1: What will your cashflow forecast look like for the next 12 months if you don't implement anything from the Blue Whale Plan?

Scenario 2: What will your cashflow forecast look like for the next 12 months, if you invest in the areas you have identified, but you only reach half of the return on investment (ROI) figures you have identified?

Scenario 3: What will your cashflow forecast look like for the next 12 months if you make the investment identified and you reach your full projection of ROI figures you identified.

Decision making

If you have a comprehensive understanding of the financial position of the business, you can make informed decisions about the direction of the business. This means that you can make strategic decisions about investments, capital expenditures and other financial matters that will drive growth.

What do we need to implement all of this effectively?

To make sure you implement all of these strategic financial goals correctly and with a good oversight and to make sure you keep control of this whole process as your business goes through this Blue Whale metamorphosis, you really need to have a comprehensive understanding of all of your financial statements. The financial statements are going to provide you with the most valuable information about the financial position of the business.

The financial statement should be produced as a minimum on a monthly basis, although you may produce several, depending on the number of areas that growth is happening in, make sure you have at least included revenue, expenses, assets and liabilities.

By analysing in detail your financial statements, you can keep track on your ROI and you can identify areas where the business is performing well and areas where it needs to improve.

Budgeting

Now we have been collecting and collating all of this financial information we must implement another important component of strategic financial management, budgeting. This budget is different from your cashflow forecast. This budget is a growth budget that takes into account your wider ambition for the business to grow rapidly now you have identified it is going to become a Blue Whale business.

This budget is a financial plan that outlines the expected revenue and expenses of the business over a three-year period, remembering that right from the start of the development of the plan, we estimated that it would take approximately three years for the business to become a Blue Whale business.

This budget should include true financial projections for the three-year period, in an informed but optimistic way, remember this part of the plan is only focussing on a future where we are hitting all of our targets and we are going to reach our full Blue Whale potential.

Use an accountant properly

Now it is time to fully brief your accountant about what you are trying to achieve. We don't want to work with an accountant who prepares your accounts annually but with whom you don't really communicate other than at this time. We need to be working with an accountant or financial specialist that understands what you are trying to achieve or even more importantly can help you fully with the growth phase.

The combination of all of these elements of strategic financial management is critical for the rapid growth phase of the Blue Whale Plan implementation in your business.

By implementing a sound financial management strategy, you can allocate resources efficiently, manage risks effectively, optimize cashflow and make informed decisions about the direction of the business.

To implement these strategic financial management goals effectively, even if you don't like working with figures, make sure you have a comprehensive understanding of financial statements, create budgets and financial projections, and work with a financial professional to implement best practices.

Sales

Another area where tracking is crucial is sales. It is vitally important that during this rapid growth period of the Blue Whale Plan that we track our sales performance to understand our customers' buying habits, identify trends in the market and adjust our sales strategies accordingly. By tracking sales, we can identify our most profitable products and services, and focus our marketing efforts on promoting those products. This will also help us to identify areas where we may be losing sales, such as poor customer service or inefficient sales processes, and make changes to address those issues.

Sales are the backbone of any business, and tracking sales outcomes and setting sales targets is an essential aspect of growing a business, during this rapid growth period of the Blue Whale Plan this is an even more important time to track sales.

Set a sales target across all aspects of your business

A sales target is a specific number or value that your sales and marketing team aims to achieve within a particular period. It is a goal that helps a business to stay focussed on its growth strategy, assess the performance of its sales team and improve its bottom line.

Tracking sales outcomes is the process of monitoring and analysing all of the sales data you are collecting to measure performance against sales targets.

This process is vital to provide insights into what works and what does not work in your sales strategy, which in turn during the raid growth phase will help your business to adjust your approach to optimize sales outcomes.

When you are tracking your sales outcomes, you really need to consider a range of metrics, including sales revenue, customer acquisition costs, conversion rates and average order value.

These sales targets are vitally important to help you and your business to set clear goals and prioritize activities to achieve those goals.

Note

All the way through the Blue Whale Plan, whether it be personal or professional, keep setting monitorable targets and solutions to ensure we keep on track, invest in a notebook that you can keep a note of your desired outcomes both personally and professionally each month, so you can tick them off as you go along.

Sales targets also provide a sense of direction and focus for your team, keeping them motivated and engaged in their work and giving them a clear outcome and a clear purpose to work toward. When setting your sales targets, you really need to consider factors such as your current sales performance, market trends and growth potential. A well-defined sales target should be specific, measurable, attainable, relevant and time-bound (SMART).

A key benefit of tracking your sales outcomes and setting your sales targets is that it allows you to identify areas for improvement. By analysing the sales data, you can identify patterns and trends in customer behaviour, such as buying habits, preferences and pain points.

These insights can help you inform ideas around product development, marketing strategies and sales techniques, enabling you and your business to better meet the needs of your customers.

Tracking sales outcomes and setting sales targets also helps your business to monitor the performance of your sales team. By regularly assessing this sales data, particularly through the rapid growth phase of the Blue Whale Plan, you can identify high-performing salespeople and areas where additional training or coaching is required. This allows your management team to provide targeted support and guidance to their team, improving their performance and ultimately driving sales growth.

Perhaps the biggest benefit of all this sales tracking to you is that it helps you to manage their resources effectively, this informs your financial tracking and helps you to develop your financial plans in a much more informed way. By setting specific targets and monitoring progress towards those targets, you can allocate your resources much more efficiently. This includes you managing staffing levels, stock levels and your marketing budgets, ensuring that all of your resources are allocated in a way that maximizes sales growth.

Competitiveness

In addition to these benefits, tracking your sales outcomes and setting sales targets can also help you and your business to stay competitive. By monitoring sales data and market trends, you can identify emerging opportunities and threats, which in turn helps you to adapt your sales strategy accordingly. This helps your business to stay ahead of the competition, maintain your market share and growing your customer base.

A word of warning

Tracking sales outcomes and setting sales targets is not without its challenges. One of the biggest challenges is ensuring that targets are realistic and achievable. Sales targets that are too ambitious can demotivate salespeople and teams, while targets that are too easy can lead to complacency and lack of effort.

To overcome this challenge, you really need to set targets that are challenging but achievable, based on a thorough understanding of yours and their sales performance and growth potential.

A secondary challenge is ensuring that all of your sales data is accurate and up to date. Sales data is only useful if it is accurate and reflects the true state of sales performance.

As we spoke about earlier in the Blue Whales Plan, this requires you and your business to implement robust data collection and analysis processes, using reliable tools and software to track and analyse sales data.

Perhaps most importantly you and your business need to ensure that they have the right skills and resources to effectively track sales outcomes and set sales targets.

It is vitally important during this rapid growth phase that you have or are building a skilled sales team, sales managers who can effectively analyse sales data, and access to the necessary tools and software to track and analyse sales data.

To reiterate

Tracking in general is vitally important for the development of the Blue Whale Plan, but tracking sales outcomes and setting sales targets is essential for growing the business. It provides you with insights into customer behaviour, helps to identify areas for improvement, enables effective resource management and ensures that businesses stay competitive in a rapidly changing marketplace, all areas that should be monitored at least on a bi weekly basis.

Stock tracking

During the Blue Whale rapid growth phase it is also essential for you if you sell physical products that you are tracking inventory levels, your business needs to ensure they have enough stock to meet customer demand without overstocking and tying up valuable resources. Stock tracking can also help you and your team identify slow-moving or obsolete products and make informed decisions about discounts or liquidation.

Stock management is an essential part of running any business. It is the process of tracking and controlling a company's stock levels to ensure that they have the right amount of stock on hand at all times. This process is crucial for businesses during the rapid growth period of the Blue Whale Plan because it can help you optimize your cashflow, reduce waste and improve customer satisfaction.

The first and most obvious benefit of tracking your stock is that it helps you avoid stockouts. A stockout occurs when a business runs out of a particular item and is unable to fulfil customer orders. Stockouts can be incredibly damaging to a business because they can result in lost sales, dissatisfied customers and damage to the company's reputation. By tracking your stock levels and reordering items before they run out, businesses can avoid stockouts and ensure that they can fulfil customer orders in a timely manner.

Tracking your stock also allows you and your business to optimize your cashflow. Holding too much stock ties up valuable resources, including cash and physical space. On the other hand, holding too little stock can result in stockouts and lost sales. By tracking stock levels, you free up cash for other purposes, such as marketing or research and development.

Another benefit of tracking stock during this rapid growth cycle of the Blue Whale Plan is that it can help you reduce waste. When your business has too much stock on hand, some of it may become obsolete or expire before it can be sold. This can result in significant losses for your business. By tracking stock levels and ordering only what is needed, you can reduce the amount of waste you generate and improve your bottom line.

Systems to track your stock

There are several tools that you can use to track your stock levels. One of the most common is a computerized inventory management system. These systems can track stock in real-time and provide you with a variety of reports and analytics that can help them make informed decisions about your stock levels.

Additionally, if you don't have one of these systems in your business and it is an investment based upon your growth, you can use manual inventory tracking methods, such as spreadsheets or pen and paper.

While these methods may be less sophisticated than computerized systems, they can still be effective for small businesses with limited inventory, which will be reviewed as the Blue Whale Plan moves towards fruition and more stock tracking is needed.

Customer satisfaction

Tracking customer satisfaction is critical for your business as it moves into this rapid growth phase of the Blue Whale Plan. It is vital for those that want to retain their customers and attract new ones. By tracking customer satisfaction, we can identify areas where we need to improve our products, services or customer service. It helps us to identify our most loyal customers and reward them for their loyalty, which can lead to increased customer retention and referrals.

By regularly measuring how satisfied your customers are with your products and services, you can gain valuable insights into what is working well and what needs improvement. This information can help you make informed decisions to increase customer loyalty, boost sales, and ultimately, grow your business.

Surveys

One of the most effective ways to track customer satisfaction is through the use of surveys. Surveys can be conducted online, over the phone or in person, and can be tailored to ask specific questions that provide meaningful feedback. Questions might cover topics such as product quality customer service, pricing and overall satisfaction with the experience of doing business with your company.

When designing a customer satisfaction survey, it is important to keep the questions simple and easy to understand. Avoid asking leading questions that might bias the responses, and give customers the option to provide open-ended feedback in addition to selecting predefined responses. This can provide more detailed insights into customer opinions and can help identify specific areas for improvement.

 Task

If you wanted to ask your customers to tell you about their perceptions of your business, what ten questions would you ask them and why? Write down those ten questions, with the knowledge of why you are asking them.

Feedback

Once you have collected customer feedback, it is important to analyse the data and identify any patterns or trends. This can be done through the use of data visualization tools or by manually reviewing the responses. Look for areas where customers consistently express dissatisfaction or areas where there are significant differences between the responses of satisfied and dissatisfied customers. This information can be used to identify specific issues that need to be addressed and to develop targeted solutions.

Customer loyalty

One of the key benefits of tracking customer satisfaction during this rapid growth phase of the Blue Whale Plan is that it can help to increase customer loyalty. When customers feel that their opinions are valued and that their feedback is being used to improve the products and services they receive, they are more likely to remain loyal to your brand, we found this through the explanation phase of plan in the dorsal fin chapter.

In fact, studies have shown that customers who are satisfied with their experience are more likely to make repeat purchases and to recommend your business to others.

Quality

Another benefit of tracking customer satisfaction is that it can help to improve the quality of your products and services. By identifying areas where customers are consistently dissatisfied, you can make targeted improvements that will improve the overall customer experience. This can help to differentiate your business from competitors and to increase customer satisfaction and loyalty over time, this is essential during this phase.

In addition to helping to improve customer satisfaction, tracking customer feedback can also provide valuable insights into market trends and customer preferences. By analysing the data collected from customer surveys, you can identify emerging trends and areas of opportunity that you might not have otherwise been aware of. This can help you to stay ahead of the curve and to develop new products and services that meet the changing needs of your customers.

Tools and strategies for effective tracking across the board

Accounting software

Accounting software, such as QuickBooks, Xero or SAGE, can help you track your finances accurately and efficiently. These tools can automate tasks such as invoicing, payroll and financial reporting, which can save you time and reduce the risk of errors. Importantly these systems can also talk directly to your accountant, making the help they can give you from a financial forecasting perspective, up to date and impactful for you gaining knowledge and investment awareness.

Customer relationship management (CRM) software

CRM software, such as Salesforce or HubSpot, can help your business track customer interactions, sales and marketing efforts. These tools can also provide insights into customer behaviour and preferences, which can help your business during this phase personalise you're marketing and sales efforts.

Stock management software

Stock management software, such as Trade Gecko or Cin7, can help your business track stock levels, sales and purchase orders. These tools can also automate tasks such as reordering and stocktaking, which can save businesses time and reduce the risk of stockouts or overstocks.

General analytics tools

Analytics tools, such as Google Analytics or Adobe Analytics, can help small businesses track website traffic, user behaviour and marketing campaigns. These tools can provide insights into the effectiveness of marketing efforts, the performance of the website, and customer behaviour, which can help businesses make data-driven decisions.

The dorsal ridge

Although this rapid growth phase is not designed to be a rollercoaster, the way that we are going to be reflective of the dorsal ridge and smooth the curve out is with all of this regular reporting and analysis.

The trick to this rapid growth process and your further development to becoming a Blue Whale business and business owner is to establish a regular reporting and analysis process to track your own and your businesses performance and critically evaluate and identify areas for improvement.

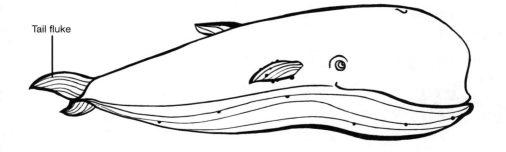

Tail fluke

Chapter 7

The tail fluke

The tail fluke of the blue whale is one of the most remarkable structures in physiology, the fluke is about 30 feet long, and it's essentially a paddle. It's used for propulsion, and it can be angled up or down to help the whale dive into deeper waters or rise to the surface.

The fluke also has a large lobe at the end, which helps it move through the water with minimal resistance. This lobe acts like an underwater rudder, helping to keep the whale on course even when it's going fast. Blue whales are capable of moving their tails at speeds up to 20 miles per hour (32 km/h).

Like the tail fluke the next part of the Blue Whale Plan is all about propulsion, whilst we have undertaken the gestation and the rapid growth phase, it is important that we can now propel both ourselves and our business in the greatest way possible.

As we move the plan forward and we keep on this trajectory to propel us to grow even faster we will all realize – and it is proven by experience – that the faster and bigger the companies and our personal capacity grows the more we will be experiencing unanticipated issues.

These issues become so important that they become not just issues but things that try to move our propulsion off course. The issues that we perceive as problems are designed to take up the space we have created through our personal growth and the businesses growth, it is very difficult to become a Blue Whale, if it was easy everyone would do it.

These issues become more of a problem because they stop us executing our plans, they take away our focus and they shout to us, "stop moving, look at me, look at me". When we do this, when we lose focus, when we stop to look, we stop growing.

This is going to sound really counterintuitive after the information contained in the previous chapters but these urgent things are usually not that important. They may feel, in the moment, like the most important thing in the world. But they aren't, and what *is* most important is rarely urgent, this is an important lesson to remember.

If you want to keep on this Blue Whale Plan path of accelerated growth, you need a system that will allow you to proactively focus on what is truly important instead of just reacting to the urgent priorities.

The Blue Whale Plan has identified four steps that will let you do just that. Following these steps will help you make sure you accomplish your biggest and most important goals and that will lead to consistent and incredible growth despite the noise.

Step 1: Focus on the goals that lead you further into the open ocean

The first step is to focus on the goals that will lead you time and time again into the open ocean, to the deeper parts of the sea. Keep the focus on what is really driving you to see these results. Remember, the urgent day-to-day issues aren't the important things.

 Task

Identify what is the one goal that, if you meet it, will make most of your other goals and ambitions irrelevant?

Once you have identified this, this is going to become your KRILL. For a Blue Whale, krill is the main source of food, the sustenance, the importance and the thing that keeps the Blue Whale moving every day. In our plan KRILL stands for: **K**nowledge, **R**esilience, **I**deation, **L**ogical and **L**eading. We discuss these five elements below.

K: Knowledge

Using knowledge in your business isn't necessarily about thinking up new products and services, or devising even more ingenious new ways of selling them, although this could be a useful tool in the KRILL process.

For this part of the process, we are going to utilize the knowledge and experience we already have in the business currently. Three areas of internal business knowledge we are going to concentrate on initially are:

1. The **experience** of the employees in the business and their openminded approaches.
2. The current **design and processes** for the goods and services we currently deliver.
3. The data we currently collect internally.

These existing forms of knowledge within our businesses are things that often we take for granted as it is the day-to-day knowledge, we use without thinking about. For the KRILL aspect of them Blue Whale Plan we are going to mindfully put this knowledge into practice.

Current market knowledge to target particular customers with specific types of products or services. Data collection from and about customers and suppliers as demonstrated during the dorsal fin part of the Plan, which can be invaluable in developing improving existing products and services.

The current team are likely to have skills and experience that we can use as an asset. Using the team's knowledge can be invaluable in setting us apart from competitors. Our understanding of what customers want, combined with our employees' know-how, is really our extensive **knowledge base** and vitally important to us as we move upwards with the Blue Whale Plan.

R: Resilience

Building resilience into the KRILL is a vital part of the Blue Whale Plan, after the COVID-19 pandemic, for all of the businesses I worked with including my own, all of the resilience plans in place were found to be somewhat lacking. This was highlighted in a number of areas, when we process the momentum of the tail fluke. How we build this momentum in, requires a concentration on several areas.

Financial resilience: The Blue Whale Plan and more specifically focussing on the KRILL output means that we need to move away from looking at short-term returns and we need to focus on long-term financial risk. We need to really balance both areas to ensure that we have a solid capital position with a sufficient amount of cashflow. This is the key to mitigating any fluctuations in revenue, cost or credit.

Technological resilience: Data and data management is the key to the success of the Blue Whale Plan, to develop resilience, your business must invest in high-quality data. You must also develop a robust IT disaster recovery plan to avoid service outages and maintain critical business operations during any disruptive event, such as a cyber-attack, which are dramatically on the rise or any similar incident.

Organizational resilience: Retaining employees with high levels of satisfaction are big parts of mastering organizational resilience, the Blue Whale Plan means that invariably change is happening, and change can lead to disruption and upset, so building resilience in the workforce is key.

Within the Krill section of the Blue Whale Plan, we must build in solutions to these three areas, to minimize disruption, to get clear employee buy-in and most importantly have a response mechanism built in to ensure that propulsion in not brought up short.

I: Ideation

Ideation is an absolutely huge component of the KRILL strategy. We have spoken about ideation in a wider context, but within the KRILL strategy we are using ideation to foster an open and honest ideas generation service to focus directly on the clearly defined KRILL output. In these circumstances, we have been using ideation techniques internally throughout the plan, now we are ging to use them externally by concentrating on our customers.

Our customers are the ones who actually *buy* and *use* our product and services, so being able to deliver what they actually want is the key to success.

Task

We are going to use customer feedback to provide us with data and information we need to make our products and services better and to keep us focussed on the KRILL outcomes.

We are going to build monthly surveys that will:

- Collect ideas about how to improve our product – what three questions will you ask?
- Explore how we will improve our customer experience and brand loyalty – which three questions will we ask and why?

When we think about the questions we may ask and we think about using ideation to keep us on track for the KRILL defined outcomes, we are going to consider four question areas.

- Ideation questions that will help us to generate ideas to improve products and services.
- Ideation questions that will help us to generate ideas for future product/service development.
- Ideation questions that will help us to generate customer feedback.
- Ideation questions that will help us to improve customer loyalty.

The ideation of the KRILL section of the Blue Whale Plan helps us to propel forwards whilst keeping on track and focussed on the clearly defined outcome we are looking to achieve.

L: Logical

When we think about the KRILL development of our Blue Whale Plan, we are reminded that we are on this propulsion path to growth as described earlier in this chapter. However, we do not want to become so myopic that we focus only on outcome and we do not then test measure and question.

There are two key logical areas that we must concentrate on, to maintain ballast and focus, alongside sense checking the conclusions we are coming up with.

- What is the opportunity we are facing, is it the same still or has it changed?
- When we think about the KRILL opportunities, we are asking ourselves on a weekly basis, is the growth opportunity still there and if it is exactly what opportunity does it present itself as?

 Task

Can you and your team answer these three questions in a positive manner (and a truthful manner) or has the way you have answered them, meant that you may need to change your approach.

1. Is the market big enough for these products or services still?
2. Do we have the right skills in our company, can we design, build, distribute and service the product or service or do we have to employ further specialists?
3. Do we have a market advantage, are we ahead of or do we need to be ahead of any current or potential rivals in the marketplace?

We should also be asking ourselves logically should we be selling new products or services to our existing customers or will we get better growth if we sell our existing products to a new customer base?

Logically as part of the KRILL process you are going to need to estimate the time needed and the cost for your business to identify a new sales prospect and then how long until they actually buy something from you.

The logic or sense check of the whole KRILL process is essential to keeping on track, keeping focussed on the outcome and a brake to becoming myopic and walking into market failure.

L: Leading

Perhaps the most important part of the whole KRILL process is your position leading the whole process. Visibly people will need to see you leading the whole process and this means keeping clarity and focus on the outcome you are trying to develop and the timescales you are trying to achieve.

This leads to you been visibly responsive in a number of areas even if you have a management team in place. Remember alongside your business you are also becoming a Blue Whale and a Blue Whale leader. Leaders with strong, trusting and authentic relationships with their teams know that investing time in building those bonds makes them more effective as a leader and creates a foundation for success. To be an effective leader you are going to have to adapt to many both internal, and external changes on this Blue Whale journey and this may mean quite often you are going to have to work outside of your comfort zone.

As we saw in the knowledge part of the KRILL process you are going to need to develop the internal knowledge function, but as leader you are also going to have to develop visibly a lifelong learning mentality within your organization. The key to all of this will be down to your agility, flexibility and adaptability, whilst spinning all of the other plates to ensure the whole organization stays on track.

It is easier said than done and sometimes you may get it wrong. The key to this will be honesty, ownership and transparency. Show every mistake, own it and then show how you are putting it right. If you foster this leadership style throughout this process, you will be further developing the focus and team honesty you are going to need to succeed.

It is possible that you already know what your KRILL should be. But it is more likely that you have so many big priorities and goals that choosing just one presents a challenge.

Perhaps even since you have started to develop your own Blue Whale Plan, you have been spending so much time dealing with urgent matters that the concept of choosing one priority goal seems overwhelming. I felt exactly the same, as I started to develop my business. It was only when I jettisoned the issues (urgent – but really non urgent issues) that the propulsion really started to take place.

If you don't know what KRILL is

If you aren't sure what your KRILL should be, I recommend you sit down with your team and make a list of all of the important priorities you want to achieve, remember it is important to get buy-in and make people part of this process. Then, isolate the two or three most critical priorities that would make the biggest impact on achieving your vision. Figure out which priority, if achieved, would catapult your organization forward the most. That's your KRILL.

Once you determine your KRILL, you need to set parameters for achieving it. Start by identifying where you are, where you want to be, and when you want to be there, even though we have done it before, they very art of repetition will make all of the difference. Define the estuary you are starting from, define the open ocean you want to reach and most importantly make sure you set a fixed deadline that everyone is aware of the is monitorable, that everyone is aware of. All KRILL must have a defined starting point a defined outcome and a defined timescale.

Step 2: Clearly define the actions you and your business will take

Remember the tail fluke is all about propulsion, so the next wave to move us forward to achieving reaching the KRILL is acting on the control measures. Control measures are the points that you control in order to achieve your end goal. To make this easier, they are the actionable things you can do today in order to influence the achievement of your KRILL result measurements.

 Task

What will be the four lead measures you and your team require that will ensure you reach the KRILL.

- How will you implement these measures?
- How will ensure focus on these measures?
- How will you be rewarded when you meet the desired outcome, using these measures?

Implementing, communicating and following these measures are the key to staying focussed, on target and most importantly bringing the whole team with you on this agreed output.

Step 3: The visual outcome board

The third step of achieving your KRILL is to keep a visual outcome board. This is needed to keep focus both for yourself and your team and also because research has shown that people reach targets and outcomes much easier when a visual and monitorable score card or outcome board is being kept.

The people in your organization are now on the Blue Whale journey, as are you and as such both ourselves and the people we are surrounding ourselves with are focussed on achieving clearly defined KRILL outcomes.

People like to have a focussed outcome, a measurable outcome to achieve. It motivates them. Without a way to keep score, people don't know if they're making progress or not, if they are doing well, or if they are doing poorly. They don't know if they're achieving the goal or falling short. Even worse, they stop caring. They become disengaged. And it is vitally important, particularly during this tail fluke portion of the plan that we keep the focus to keep the propulsion moving forwards.

To be effective, your KRILL outcome board must be designed and controlled by the players themselves. The outcome board should be highly visible, compelling and simple to follow. It must reflect accurate measures, as well as a focus for each team or team member on how they reach the KRILL target in a measurable way.

When looking at the outcome board – in whichever way you and the team constructs the outcome board to be – each team member should know exactly where they stand and where each of the other team members stands. It should be easy to see if they are achieving or not.

Step 4: Food chain accountability

The thing to remember about KRILL and the Blue Whale. KRILL is the Blue Whale's source of food. If the Blue Whale doesn't have KRILL it doesn't survive. We have a very, very hungry largest mammal in the world.

We need to hold both ourselves and our teams accountable to executing the correct measures to accomplish us reaching the KRILL. Monitoring and conversation and buy-in is central to the success of the propulsion phase. Visible accountability is a powerful motivation tool, to ensure propulsion is maintained and a sense of ownership is conveyed between yourself and the team.

 **Task**

We suggest a KRILL session meeting either online or a face-to-face meeting on a weekly basis where each team member reports on their success or failure in meeting the commitments they made during the previous week's meeting.

The KRILL session is held on the same day and time each week and nothing other than the achievement of the KRILL is mentioned during the meeting. The entire focus of this meeting is accountability for propelling forwards.

Start off every meeting by reminding the team of the KRILL outcome you all agreed upon and set as a target and uncover what progress has been made to date, and whether the group is on track with the KRILL measurable outcomes.

After all of the members of the meeting finish reporting on their results, we then recap all of the KRILL measures and then make two commitments for what they will accomplish in the coming week.

The benefit to these KRILL meetings are twofold. Not only will this help the team focus on the KRILL goals, importantly it will continue to highlight the benefits of reaching the long-term goal.

To keep the momentum of the Blue Whale Plan and its propulsion it is important to create an alignment and relationships that build when team members hold each other accountable and the whole team including yourself operate with transparency.

Meeting consistently every week and working together to achieve the KRILL goal is a really powerful and tremendous team-building tool.

KRILL is the largest tool to achieve your rapid growth

Regardless of your industry or the size and maturity of your business, using these four steps on the Blue Whale Plan to implement the KRILL outcomes will absolutely transform both you and your business.

Because you and the team have identified the KRILL, the single most important priority and how they fit into achieving that priority, every single person is on the same page. That, in and of itself, is extremely powerful and very reflective of all the Blue Whale companies I have worked with.

Because this four-step process includes an accountability factor, there's no chance that the important priority will fall through the cracks, even when those other priorities that seem urgent.

Consistently using these four steps during the tail fluke stage of the Blue Whale Plan will help you and your business to propel along a path of exponential, accelerated growth, with a clear focus on the open ocean.

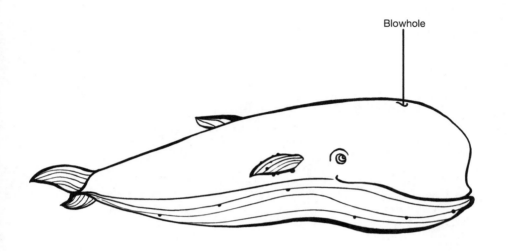

Blowhole

Chapter 8

The blowhole

The blowhole of the blue whale is not just a hole. It is, in fact, an organ that enables the whale to breathe while it's underwater. The blowhole is located at the top of the whale's head and can be used as a way to release excess heat from its body.

The blue whale has two blowholes on either side of its head, which allows it to breathe in two different directions simultaneously. This is important because it allows them to take in more air than other types of whales that only have one blowhole.

The blue whale also has a unique way for expelling water from its mouth after it has taken in air through its blowhole. Instead of blowing bubbles out like most other marine mammals do, it uses something called "ventilation" or "ventilating". This means that when the whale exhales through its nose or mouth instead of releasing bubbles into the water, it blows them directly into its lungs where they will remain until they need them again, then they'll be expelled with another breath.

The blowhole is about three feet in diameter, but for a whale that can reach up to 100 feet long (and weigh anywhere from 200 to 300 tons), this is understandable. The blue whale typically blows air out of its blowhole every few minutes; however, when it's swimming quickly or diving deep into cold water, it will take longer than usual to exhale air from its lungs through its only hole.

In the context of us and our business being the Blue Whale, we are identifying the ways we communicate to the world to help us tell our story, to leverage our size, to share our experience and most importantly reach new customers and markets both nationally and internationally.

In the blowhole analogy, we are literally spraying a huge jet of information out into the world, however, unlike the water expelled from the blowhole, we care where this hits, where it lands and most importantly who gets wet!

Let's consider first the case for creating and developing the business on an international stage, whether or not in these early stages of Blue Whale Plan development you want to trade on that basis.

Why we should look to the world to become a Blue Whale

When we look at the growth cycle of any individual or business in this new globalized world, we can spot both learning opportunities and business opportunities. Interestingly, the pandemic heightened our ability to spot these opportunities without travel and lead more businesses to explore what this could mean to them.

Increasingly, global trade barriers are disappearing and what's left is a connected world where it can be as easy to do work on a nomadic basis rather than be based in a particular spot.

Internationalization is a process that involves expanding your business activities beyond your domestic borders to tap into the global market and for businesses looking to expand their customer base and boost their revenue, and importantly as we talk about profile and reach, internationalization is the way to go.

This global approach does two things immediately, it both increases yours and your businesses visibility and done well it also increases your customer base.

As we expand our business activities beyond our domestic borders, we expose our products and services to a much larger market. We can attract new customers and tap into new markets that were previously inaccessible. By targeting these new markets, we can also diversify our customer base and reduce our dependence on a single market.

This is very important on our journey to becoming Blue Whales as this reduces the risk to us of market fluctuations and helps us to maintain stable revenue streams and revenue opportunities.

Task

Identify three products or services you currently deliver as part of your business that you think would be the best products or services to promote on a global basis.

Why did you pick these products?

What data did you base this decision on?

What makes you feel most passionate about these products or services?

Internationalizing our business helps us to increase our revenue

By expanding our business activities into new markets, we can tap into new sources of revenue. We can increase our market share, sell more products and services, and generate more revenue.

This also allows you to take advantage of economies of scale by producing in larger quantities and reducing our unit costs if we sell products or offer our services on a basis which is easy to replicate. This will help us to improve our profit margins and increase our bottom line.

We will discuss further in the chapter about tips and techniques to attract more customers in these new markets but importantly having and maintain this focus throughout the Blue Whale process will help us to develop and deliver the managed growth and success we are looking for.

Brand image and letting the world identify us

Building a brand that helps us to be identified on a world stage is key to the success, not only to the international adventure but also to lift and raise our profile on both a local and national basis.

When we expand our business activities into new markets, we can improve our brand image and reputation. This really helps us to differentiate ourselves from our competitors, build customer loyalty and increase our market share. A positive brand image can also help us to attract new customers, investors and partners.

 Task

Identifying the key components of our brand image – what matters?

When we think about our brand image we are really going back to the point of building and developing and most importantly demonstrating and verbalizing our brand values.

How would you describe your business?

For any content you put out there about your business, there are six areas that you need to consider when you're creating it.

If you weren't in the room and your current customers were, how would they describe you brand values or brand image? Have you ever asked them?

What is it that makes your company and brand stand out from everyone else?

What is it that makes you different and that you love to do? Identify four key areas.

> What qualities within your business, product or service are you most proud of?
>
> What one word would you use to describe your product or service?

Learning and education

Identifying opportunities and learning on a global basis really helps us not just to identify new opportunities and growth, it builds our confidence and opens our minds to new ways to present our business locally as well as nationally. By expanding our business activities into new markets, we learn from different cultures, business practices and customer preferences. This is vital to help us move towards increased longevity and growth, and it can help us to improve our product or service design, marketing strategies and customer service. We can also learn new ways of doing business that can help us to improve our competitiveness and profitability.

This really helps us to reduce our dependence on domestic markets, and this is a key component of the Blue Whale Plan, to spread risk, to increase capacity and most importantly open up new routes of market.

By expanding our business activities into new markets, we reduce our dependence on domestic markets that may be volatile or subject to economic downturns. This is important during these growth cycles to help us to maintain a stable revenue stream and improve our business resilience. The process of telling the world we have arrived and are no longer the biggest animal the world has ever seen but also the most clandestine.

So, the blowhole is all about letting the world know about us. From a Blue Whale perspective, the blowhole and the jet of expelled water it projects into the outside world is perhaps the only way we ever identify that the whale is indeed there, below the waves.

Areas to think about on the Blue Whale journey to let the world know we are here

It's now time for us to be less secretive and move out into the water in a way which easily identifies who we are and what we do. We can do this in many ways but we really should be concentrating on the brand building ability in this global ocean and the impact we can make.

Building a strong online presence

In this Blue Whale process, having a strong online presence is crucial for growing the business, the businesses reputation and also your presence and reputation.

So, we know that you already have an online presence, you wouldn't be running your business successfully without one, but how do we maximize this? How do we tell the world we have arrived and most importantly how do we do this in a way that opens more potential sales channels and opportunities.

Develop your website further

 Task

Take a look at your website with new eyes. Give your website to a 10-year-old child and ask them to navigate their way around it. Give them some specific items, products or services they must find and ask them to do it in no more than three clicks. Is it possible?

Now repeat the process with a 20-year-old person and a 50-year-old person. Are the answers the same? Have they identified areas for improvement?

How accessible are you online?

The first steps to becoming much more visible start with your website. I like to think of your website in this way. Do you remember the book or the film of *The Lion, the Witch and the Wardrobe*? When you walked through the wardrobe it was a portal into a whole new world, Narnia. You should think of your website as your wardrobe. When somebody enters it do you take them to Narnia (the joys of your business world) or do you take them to the back of the wardrobe?

Your website should be easy to navigate, visually appealing and mobile-friendly. Your website is a real reflection of your business, so it must represent your brand and provide relevant information about your products or services, but most importantly it must be the Narnia of your business, full of wonder, interest, intrigue and perhaps most of all opportunity. Now reviewing your website is it Narnia or just the back of a wardrobe?

Optimize your website for users and search engines

It's wonderful to have created Narnia as your website, but if Lucy, Edmund and all of the other visitors can't actually find the wardrobe, well what is the point? Search engine optimization (SEO) is essential to ensure your website appears on the first page of search results, forget any page other than the first, you will never find the wardrobe.

It's a murky world the world of SEO, but there are ways for you to be educated and informed on the purpose of it, indeed should be informed about it, especially if this is something you are outsourcing as part of your business. Don't forget the focus of this whole process is the creation of the blowhole, the development of becoming hidden no more.

When searching online for a definition of SEO, this is the best I could come up with "Using relevant keywords, meta tags, and descriptions to improve your website's ranking on search engines like Google".

But SEO is so much more

There are several areas where SEO becomes not only the key to the growth of your website's traffic it can also inform and help you to target your traditional marketing outcomes in a new way.

The first step in any SEO strategy is to conduct keyword research. Keyword research involves identifying the words and phrases that your target audience is searching for online. By optimizing your website for these keywords, you can improve your chances of appearing in search engine results pages (SERPs) when people search for them.

But think about this, if your customers are using these words to find you online, they will also be using these words to find you offline also.

 Task

Conduct some keyword research both online and offline.

For our online keywords we can use tools like Google Keyword Planner, Ahrefs and SEMrush to identify the words people are using and searching for, for like-minded products, businesses or services.

Offline we can very simply ask our customers to list ten words that describe our business, our products or our services.

Once we have identified our target keywords, we can begin to both optimize our website for them and also begin reviewing and redeveloping any traditional marketing collateral this may affect.

We must remember to incorporate the keywords into our website's content, including titles, headings and meta descriptions. If we are using a specialist to do this, having this knowledge allows us to project during this growth process an air of knowledge and also a focus on what we are looking to achieve when paying for the service.

Create quality content

Its ok to have a great wardrobe, but if the Narnia beyond it is dull and boring, no talking animals, witches, etc., then what's the point of the magical wardrobe. Creating quality content is the most effective way to attract and retain customers.

The content we create to populate the website, the messaging we put out and the conversations we have with our customers both on and offline should be relevant, informative and engaging.

 Weekly task

In your business, identify where the quality content is and who is producing it?

Think about things such as: blog posts, articles, videos, stories, PR and everywhere the content of your business is created.

Now with a critical eye, if you were a customer, which of this content would have a direct impact on you and your life?

Does your content tell the world about you and your business, or does it add value to your current or potential customers?

What should quality content look like for you and your business?

Social media

Social media platforms like Facebook, Twitter, Instagram, LinkedIn, TikTok, etc., provide businesses with an opportunity to connect with customers and increase brand awareness.

However – and here is the buyer beware warning – creating a presence on all platforms and doing it badly is a way to hamper this process from the start. It is much more beneficial to create non generic social media content that adds value and attracts customers and purchases on one platform before moving to the next.

If someone is managing this creative social process for you, there must be brand alignment across all of the engaged platforms, but a differentiated content approach to all of the platforms is essential.

Social media done well, from a Blue Whale perspective, is not a one size fits all or a scatter gun approach.

A strategy for growth and visibility

We are going to assume that in 2023 and beyond, that you and your business have at least heard of social media and are using at least one platform.

For our Blue Whale purposes in terms of letting the world know who we are and what we do, we are going to focus on creating a strategy to build and grow market share and awareness. To do this we are going to, as we have with our whole sales process up until this point, really clearly define our objectives and the KPI outcomes we are looking to achieve.

Is our goal to drive website traffic, increase sales or build brand awareness? Having a clear understanding of our objectives will help us to design an effective strategy, which like all parts of the Blue Whale process is data driven and easily monitorable.

Clearly defining the KPIs we are looking to achieve, such as click-through rates, conversion rates and ROI, will also help us to measure the success of the social media process and to make longer term decisions on investment and potential advertising spend.

This process as with everything in the Blue Whale Plan is designed to help us make both informed and data-driven decisions.

Weekly task

Identify three key metrics that you consider will constitute success by using social media to grow the business and increase it awareness.

Identifying the key audience

Perhaps the best thing about social media platforms is that as a business it is possible to access the platforms and advanced targeting options for free. This is the key to allowing us to reach our ideal audience with precision.

Instead of targeting everyone on the platform, we can use targeting features to hone in on users who are most likely to be interested in our business, our products or our services.

The free targeting options include demographic targeting, interests targeting, behaviour targeting and lookalike targeting. By using this free service of audience targeting, we can maximize our reach and most importantly our meaningful engagement by reaching the right people with the right message.

 Task

Identify five target potential customer groups by:

- Demographic
- Interests
- Behaviour
- Location
- Building a lookalike customer using your current customer makeup.

Remember the wardrobe

Social media can drive traffic to your website, and this is very important. The data you collect outside of the platforms is where your growth and income are.

Remember any social media platform, owns the data you are creating, only by creating customer data off platform can we own that data ourselves and this is key to growth happening.

So, if our website is the wardrobe and the content is Narnia, then the real traffic driven by social media platform to our website is the real magic and this happens as they open the door to the wardrobe, the landing pages.

We know from the previous work we have done, that during this growth process we have to ensure that our landing pages are optimized for conversion by having clear calls to action, user-friendly design and relevant content.

It is essential to monitor and adjust our content to respond to a changing world and a changing social media landscape. As with all of the process just as we discovered in the dorsal fin chapter, we must monitor the metrics that matter most to our business, such as conversion rates and ROI, there is no point developing this as a strategy and marketing tool to let the world know about our journey to becoming a Blue Whale, if we are not reaching those we need to.

Now we have email addresses lets leverage email marketing to get noticed

Throughout this whole Blue Whale process at its essence in terms of driving growth and visibility has been, the power of data collection and providing a clear and consistent message to the world.

Email marketing is an effective and efficient way to do this. Not only is this a cost-effective marketing strategy, but it is also a strategy that helps create more informed customer data, habit data and perhaps most importantly buying data and attitudes.

Compared to traditional marketing methods, email marketing is much cheaper and it allows us to reach a large number of people with just one email in a highly targeted way. By using email marketing, we can further segment our email lists and send personalized messages to specific groups of people. This is so powerful during this growth process and beyond, this means we can tailor our messages to suit the specific interests and needs of our audience.

This not only increases the effectiveness of our marketing message, but it also helps to build stronger relationships with customers. When customers feel that we as a business understand their needs and interests, they are more likely to remain loyal to us, recommend others to us and engage with our content.

 Task

Identify which category specific email lists you have in your business.

Do they correspond to the five areas we looked at and identified in the social media section?

Do you need to reclassify your email lists and break them down to ensure effective marketing?

Like social media, this email marketing approach is not a one size fits all approach.

Measurement

As with everything we are developing within the plan, the data we are creating and the results of that data is essential. By using email marketing, we can measure our marketing success. We can track how many people have opened their emails, clicked on links and taken action. This data allows us to measure the effectiveness of our marketing campaigns and make adjustments as needed alongside help us to build our brand.

By using email marketing, testing and measuring and most importantly using consistent branding in our emails, we are reinforcing our brand identity and increasing our brand awareness. Each step of the way we are building a data driven growth plan, to extend our reach to customers, our reach to the world and we are becoming more and more visible.

Perhaps importantly throughout this process we must also mention that most of this data driven marketing approach can be automated. This means that we can set up automated email campaigns that are triggered by specific actions, such as when a customer makes a purchase or signs up for a newsletter.

A funnel or a click funnel can be the difference to a sale and an ongoing relationship rather than a one-time purchase limited by reach. These funnels and automated email campaigns are a great way to keep in touch with customers and keep them engaged with our brand and it not only saves time, but it also ensures that customers are receiving relevant and timely messages, and we are targeting people with the right message at the right time.

Analytics

Throughout this Blue Whale Plan, we have talked about data and data driven solutions to achieve this rapid growth after a period of stagnation and analytic based tools are the key to this.

Testing, measuring and importantly understanding the metrics we are creating in letting the world know, who and what we do and sell are the key to establishing this growth but more importantly in this instance letting the world know exactly who we are.

Rising to the surface and using the blowhole

The power of this whole process and letting the world recognize what your business is and what it does cannot be overstated.

To become a true Blue Whale, we really need to be operating in a global economy that is increasingly interconnected and competitive, challenging ourselves and having a clear data driven and compelling identity will make all of the difference.

When the world knows consistently who we are, what our business is all about and what we stand for, we can attract customers, partners, investors and employees who share your values and vision. This is the key to growth, to us building a strong brand and reputation, generating buzz and excitement, and achieving sustainable growth over the long term.

In a globally dominated marketplace, even on a local level our customers have more choices than ever before, and they are often overwhelmed by the sheer volume of products and services available to them.

When our business is recognized in the world, customers are more likely to trust us, because they know that we have a track record of delivering high-quality products and services that meet their needs, they are more likely to recommend us to others, which helps us to build a loyal customer base and increase your market share.

As we grow and develop and move along this process – this Blue Whale growth – and being noticed means that it will become easier to attract partners and investors. But this won't happen if we stay discreet, under the water and far from the surface.

When our business is known for its expertise and leadership in a particular industry or field, we can attract partners who share our vision and can help us to achieve our goals. If we build it, they will come.

It's important that we remember that we are the growth catalyst, but we can also attract investors who are interested in supporting our growth and helping us take our business to the next level. When investors see that our businesses are recognized in the world, they are more likely to believe in our potential and invest in our future.

This visibility process helps us to attract and retain top talent. We will be recognized and known for our values, culture and mission, and this is the key to attracting employees who share your passion and commitment. But we have to be visible to do it.

Throughout this Blue Whale process, we are looking to build and expand upon businesses that will be known for their excellence, innovation and impact, we are building brands that people trust and admire.

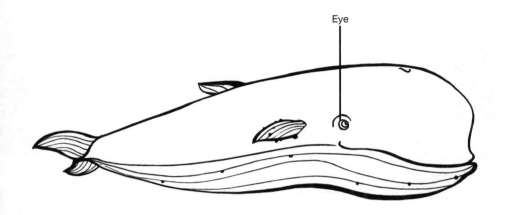

Eye

Chapter 9

The eye

The eye of a blue whale is one of the largest eyes found in the animal kingdom. It is about the size of a grapefruit, measuring up to 3.5 inches (9 cm) in diameter. The size of the eye is proportional to the body size of the blue whale.

The blue whale's eye is adapted to life in the deep ocean. The pupil can dilate and contract to allow the whale to adjust to changes in light levels as it moves from the surface to deeper waters. The whale also has a reflective layer in the back of its eye, called the tapetum lucidum, which helps to increase its sensitivity to light and improve its night vision.

The blue whale's eye is protected by a thick layer of tissue, called the blubber, which surrounds its head. This helps to insulate the eye from the cold water and cushion it from any impacts.

Watching out for icebergs

Within the Blue Whale Plan, whilst we are moving toward growth, sustaining growth, developing growth and becoming more and more visible, the eye of the blue whale is very important.

Markets – and the world – changes and often we have little or no control or influence over those changes and developments. We call those changes the icebergs, and the largest eye in the world becomes the key to our business not becoming the blue whale version of the titanic.

But how do we do that?

How do we watch out for these things that we have little or no control over? How do we develop the skills to anticipate and navigate the icebergs in the water? How do we manage change within these businesses as changes internally and in effect internal icebergs are as much of a problem as the external icebergs?

From a change perspective many of the Blue Whale businesses can hit these icebergs and struggle with internal and external change because it seems much more important to just "swim on" – focussing on reaching the end goal or target without looking around.

There are several elements we must consider to manage this change process. The overall goal remains the same within this process, but avoiding icebergs will be an inevitable part of this change process.

Depending on how old you are, you may remember an old arcade game called "Frogger". The aim of the game was for you to get your frog across the road safely and to avoid being hit by either a car, a truck or even a log, once you got safely to the other side, you had to repeat the process to cross again. The change process or the iceberg avoiding process is the Blue Whale version of this game. As things grow internally and externally, there are a number of processes you will likely recognize that need to be repeated.

This ongoing phase can be a massively challenging time, as it requires you to be on iceberg alert to navigate through various channels and make critical decisions on a basis which is often predicated on future plans or ambitions.

One of the most important decisions a company needs to make during the growth phase is setting a vision for change. Do have déjà vu yet? Didn't we discuss vision at the beginning of the book during the Gestation period? Why would we be repeating the process again, I know where I am heading, I am just trying to avoid the icebergs.

Here's why it is important to reset your vision during each part of the growth process.

> A vision is a clear and inspiring statement that describes what the company wants to achieve in the future. It is a tool that helps align the company's goals and objectives, provides direction, and motivates employees to work towards a common goal.

Recognize this statement above?

Absolutely you do, this is the starting point for the whole Blue Whale Plan. However, whilst we have been setting and following that vision the world has changed, both internally and externally.

If the Blue Whale Plan is working and we are seeing growth in your business, you will be employing more staff members, working with more suppliers, introducing systems and developing a global approach. These people and organizations have joined your journey, they are not the same people who were involved in your start phase. They need to understand what each part of this growth journey looks like.

Setting a vision is crucial during this phase of business growth because it helps everyone to stay focussed on long-term goals while dealing with the day-to-day challenges of expansion and to buy-in – or rediscover the hoped for and worked toward outcome.

Once you have identified where change has happened and will happen in the next part of the growth process, the next step is to re-define the vision, to take into account what the vision looked like at the start and how that vision looks now.

This re-vision, vision should be a clear and describe the journey still to travel, whilst acknowledging the change and development that will still be needed to make this vision achievable. This clear definition of the re-vision is essential to be communicated to not only those new to the journey, but essentially to those that have embarked on the Blue Whale Plan journey with you from the start. This is crucial because the success of the vision depends on how well it is understood and embraced.

Develop your change strategy

Developing your change strategy as part of the Blue Whale Plan is a critical step towards avoiding the icebergs and staying on track in clear blue ocean. The change strategy should help to navigate the complex-ities and challenges that come with implementing change and growth development.

Now we have re-defined our vision and objectives, the next step is to conduct a gap analysis. This really means assessing and being critical of the current state of our business, being open and honest about what is working and what isn't and then identifying the gaps between its current state and our desired end state. This analysis will help us to identify the areas that need to be addressed and the changes that need to be made to avoid those pesky icebergs.

Send in the whalers

It's an awful analogy, but the reason that the blue whale almost became extinct was because of the success of the whaling industry. Those who were adept at identifying the habit and migration paths of the blue whale were the best at almost driving them to extinction. And yet for the Blue Whale Plan purposes the success of any change initiative depends on having the right people in place (the "whalers").

As part of the change strategy process, we will need to assemble a team of individuals who have the necessary skills, experience and authority to drive the change process forwards.

Usually the "whalers" – or the change management team as they probably should be known – should include participants from all business areas, as well as any necessary external consultants or experts.

This whole process will start to build new icebergs on the journey. Change initiatives always come with risks, and it is important to identify and manage these risks throughout the change process. This includes developing a strong contingency plan for potential issues and proactively addressing any issues or icebergs that arise.

Developing a strong contingency plan (what if we need to avoid more than icebergs?)

When we are thinking about developing our contingency plan as part of our overall proactive approach we are really planning to be prepared for unexpected events.

This is our roadmap that outlines the steps we will take when we go on this journey to growth and development. Our ambition with the whole "eye" process is to minimize any impact on our businesses and ensure our continuity and vision progress.

 Task

Can you identify any potential icebergs on the journey at this time?

Think about where you started and the things you have encountered so far. As we implement the Blue Whale Plan will these icebergs get bigger but remain the same icebergs in essence or will we be looking at whole new ice problems?

We are going to categorize those risks into internal and external factors. To give you some examples and to help you identify where these icebergs may happen.

Internal factors

These may include things such as high employee turnover, system failures and supply chain disruptions which would prevent you getting your product or service to market on time or with time to spare.

External factors

These may include things like natural disasters, pandemics and economic downturns.

Task

As part of this task, can you identify six internal and six external factors that you may categorize as icebergs on this Blue Whale journey?

Once you have identified each of the six, now please prioritize them based on their likelihood and impact on your business.

You are now in the process of building a contingency plan. This process should be repeated at least six monthly, but always when an iceberg has been spotted some way off in the ocean.

Iceberg strategies

The next step in our Blue Whale Plan process is to develop a strategy or multiple strategies to mitigate the risks we have identified and ranked.

When you are thinking about these strategies, you may want to consider areas such as investing in backup systems, developing alternative supply chain channels or implementing remote work policies. These strategies should be developed based on the six icebergs you clearly defined previously.

 Task

Having clearly defined the iceberg issues, can you identify what strategies you will need to put in place to overcome them.

Make sure to include any internal and external factors and importantly think about how you will fund and implement this process throughout your business.

Implement the change plan overall

With the change plan in place, it is time to implement the change. Now we need to communicate the plan again, execute the plan, monitor progress and make adjustments as needed.

Importantly, the icebergs that we have identified will come and go and be replaced by others along the journey so it is essential that we keep a watchful eye on the ocean at all times and revisit this process often.

Whilst we are embarking on this change journey, it is vital to consider how ready we are for the whole process.

Don't be so large as a Blue Whale that you are unable to change course and continue to move ahead without looking around and using those huge eyes. As a Blue Whale leader, you must be prepared to change course, to be flexible and most importantly listen to and learn from others. Do not just carry on ahead in the vague hope that energy or willpower will overcome whatever lies ahead.

Remember, this process will also bring conflict internally, be mindful of how your teams and the other committed participants on this journey are and whilst not shying away from the conflict that change brings, minimize this with good and clear communication, with a clearly communicated vision and purpose and most importantly with a Blue Whale attitude to use those eyes to watch, learn and build from other members of this Blue Whale pod.

It is important to communicate and demonstrate both verbally and non-verbally just how important this process is and how valued each member of the Blue Whale pod are.

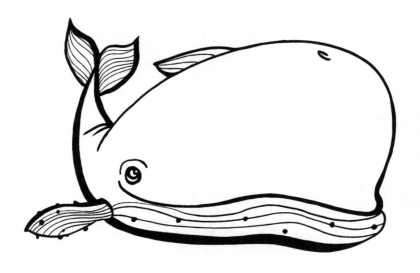

Chapter 10

Size and growth

The Blue Whale is the largest creature to have ever lived. On average Blue Whales weigh around 150 tons and are often more than 30 meters in size. To put his into context for you, the length of a Blue Whale is like having three double decker busses lined up, with a Mini Cooper at the end. Talking about Mini Coopers, a Blue Whales heart is the size of a small car – that is huge!

For us, as both Blue Whale individuals and Blue Whale businesses, that could become a problem, both internally and externally whilst we are on this personal and professional growth journey, we are communicating our purpose to employees, stakeholders, investors, customers and the world.

It makes for an interesting journey and one hopefully lots of people are buying into, but it is important to remember that sometimes this growth will not just be impressive, sometimes it may be stratospheric, however at other times, growth will be stilted and not quite meet the vision we are trying to reach.

It is very important that we manage the expectations of all involved, including ourselves, to keep the size on track, to keep the team on track and perhaps most importantly, to keep ourselves on track.

Let's talk about managing expectations and why expectations need to be managed. We have set out on this journey, we have a plan, we have started to implement the plan, we have everyone on board and we have told the world what we are doing.

We have the website, who we think are the right people in place, the stakeholders, the social media, the PR, the recognition and most importantly we have the right Blue Whale mindset and it is going well for a while and then growth slows or even stalls.

Slow or stalled growth

When we were watching out for the icebergs we talked about internal and external expectations and bringing everyone along whilst avoiding any potential mistakes and we will revisit internal and external expectations, but it is important to realize that the pace of growth is very significant both internally and externally.

Starting on this Blue Whale journey can be an exciting endeavour, and it is important to highlight your business, alongside those that already know how to build, grow and sustain a successful business.

We now re-focus on nurturing the business and ourselves to be all we can be. Be under no illusion that the Blue Whale process can be a challenging one. It will be very easy to look for comfort and look backwards and say, we didn't used to do it like this, we used to be so much happier, shall we go back to how things were?

While all of us starting on this journey of personal and professional growth will be dreaming of achieving this right away, the reality is that this is not always the case. Sometimes, despite your best efforts, the growth of your business may be slower than expected. In such situations, managing your expectations is critical to avoid feeling discouraged or defeated.

One of the first things to keep in mind when facing slow business growth is that it is not necessarily a reflection of your abilities or the quality of your product or service. There could be many reasons why your business is not taking off as fast as you expected.

As we discovered when trying to identify the icebergs that we may find along the way, some of these factors could be external, such as market conditions, competition or economic downturns, others could be internal, such as marketing strategies, ineffective sales techniques or inadequate financial planning. Regardless of the reasons behind slow business growth, it is important to manage our expectations by setting realistic goals and timelines.

Let's revisit our goals and break them down into smaller more manageable goals to ensure that we are not setting ambitious targets and projections that are just too difficult to meet in one go as this can lead to disappointment and frustration if these goals are not met. Instead, let's take a step back and assess your current situation objectively.

We are going to revisit our sales figures, customer feedback and market trends to get a better sense of where we stand and what you can realistically achieve in the short and long term.

 Task

Write down the large goal you are trying to achieve by becoming a Blue Whale business. So, as an example, you may have written something like:

> In five years, I will have grown my business, from £100,000 turnover to £5 million turnover and I will have 100 employees and be providing my product or service in 30 countries across the world.

Now we are going to revisit that goal and split it into several smaller more manageable goals, more achievable goals and most importantly more focussed goals.

So, for example, you might have split that large goal into a set of goals that focusses on particular areas, such as:

> In year one of trying to develop the business from where it is now, we will increase the turnover from £100,000 to £1 million.

> To do this we need to increase our customer base from X to X ensuring that all of our customers, buy another product from us within at least three months of purchasing the previous product.

Do you see the difference?

> The overall goal remains exactly the same £100,000 to £5 million and yet by splitting it down to more manageable sections, slow growth does not seem the catastrophic event it would if you were continuously having the large target as your main focus.
>
> The task for you now is to take the large goal you have just written down and split it into ten smaller more manageable time sensitive versions of that goal.

Once we start setting these more realistic and achievable goals and timelines that take into account any challenges or limitations we may be facing, without taking our very large eye off the overall goal, the focus suddenly becomes keener and more achievable.

However, when we are dealing with slow business growth we need to stay actively and visibly positive and focussed on the big picture, even if we are not feeling that way. Remember our Blue Whale size now dictates that people will be interested in following our story and following our progress.

It can be easy to get bogged down in day-to-day challenges and setbacks, but it is important to keep your eyes on the prize and remind yourself why we started this journey in the first place.

Stay motivated by celebrating small wins, and small targets leading to the bigger outcomes and see these successes as stepping stones to reach your larger goals, talk about them, share the journey and most of all to get into buy in to this Blue Whale process share the journey.

Surround yourself with other whales

It doesn't so much matter if they are humpback, blue, killer, grey or even narwhale, one of the best ways to stay on track and focussed is to surround yourself with a strong support system and like-minded and encouraging individuals.

This supportive network of mentors, peers and advisors can provide guidance, encouragement and constructive feedback along your journey, likely you will be providing the same service to them. These pods of whales can come from anywhere, but the most important aspect is that they share your passions for both personal and professional growth.

Finding your pod

When we think about building our pod, it is important to think about the type of pod we are building. In our Blue Whale analogy, building a pod of only Blue Whales would be amazing, it does mean that you are swimming with a pod that thinks looks and acts exactly the way you do.

By building a diverse pod, of differing whales, differing experience, talents and focus, you are challenging yourself, learning new things and most importantly opening up that huge Blue Whale brain to new experiences and learning.

Define your needs

The first step in identifying this supportive pod of mentors, peers and advisors is to define your needs. Take an inventory of your strengths and weaknesses and identify the areas where you need the most support. Some of the key areas to consider include:

- **Technical skills:** How strong are your analytical skills, are you an entrepreneur with lots of good ideas but you move from thing to thing, or are you analytical with an eye for details, consider which are your strengths and weaknesses.
- **Soft skills:** These are the interpersonal skills required to build relationships with customers, partners and employees, such as communication, leadership and teamwork.

- **Industry expertise:** This is the knowledge and experience required to navigate the specific industry in which you plan to grow and develop or new industry areas you may spot opportunities in and may want to focus on.

 Task

Make an honest list of all of your clearly identifiable strengths and write it down, taking into account, your technical skills, soft skills and industry expertise.

Now make an opposite list of all of the weaknesses you feel you may hold.

This is the pool of whales we are going to build our pod from.

How do we find the pod?

Once we have clearly identified the backgrounds of the members of our pod, it is time to put some faces to the backgrounds. We must be really clear here and recognize that sometimes a humpback whale and a blue whale will just not get on, so do not be disheartened if all of the whales you identify in this first instance do not want to join your pod, swim further in the ocean to find even more whales to consider.

There are several areas we may be able to find and identify the members of our pod from to give us a swimming start.

- **Professional organizations:** These are organizations that bring together professionals in a specific industry or field. They often offer networking events, mentorship programs and other resources to help members advance their careers.

- **Business accelerators:** These are organizations and are often based within universities that provide resources and support to help businesses grow and accelerate. They often offer mentorship programs, networking events and other resources to help entrepreneurs reach their potential.
- **Online communities:** These are online forums and groups where you can connect with peers, mentors and advisors from around the world.

They often offer a wealth of knowledge, advice and support to help entrepreneurs overcome challenges and achieve their goals but more importantly they offer view points from across the globe which is very valuable as we build our international Blue Whale business.

 Task

Research and write down five organizations, accelerators or online communities within a 50-mile radius of where you are based.

Join all five for an initial meeting within the next 30 days.

Be specific about the makeup of the pod

Now we have joined these groups and are looking for the exact make up of how our surrounding group should be when we identify those members, we think would be good we need to start evaluating their experience, expertise and track record to determine whether they are a good fit for our needs. Some of the key factors to consider include:

- **Experience:** Think about the number of years of experience a mentor, peer or advisor has in your industry or field. The more experience they have, the more valuable their insights and advice are likely to be. But. And here is a word of caution, with experience also can come complacency. You already have a business and business experience, but are talking it from where it was and has been for a time period, to beyond your past expectations. Try to avoid those with a similar set of experience to you before you started this journey. Their role without them knowing it, could be to drag you back to where you were when this process started.

- **Expertise:** Think about the specific skills, knowledge and expertise a mentor, peer or advisor has in your area of need. Think about the list you made on the previous task identifying your areas of skills and the weaknesses you identified, be specific that members of the pod, fulfil and make up for these clearly identified skill weakness areas.

- **Track record:** Think about the success and accomplishments of a mentor, peer or advisor. You should look for candidates who have a track record of success in an industry or field that complements the needs you have in building your pod.

 Task

In the next 30 days whilst attending these events both online and offline, build a list of no less than 20 names of people you think would be good for your pod, and start to arrange meetings to discuss your needs but also their needs to see if there is any pod synergy or if indeed you like or get a warm feeling about their participation.

Be honest about your needs and goals, and be open to feedback and advice, show respect for the time and knowledge of your mentors, peers and advisors and most importantly, give as much back as you receive to your group you build.

A word of warning

Watch out for the Killer Whales, they can often disrupt your pod and be a member for the wrong reasons. People like this, should not become a permanent member of your pod.

Adapting your business strategy as a result of the work you have undertaken so far. When we are experiencing this period of slow business growth it is important to be open to pivoting or adapting our business strategy if needed. Sometimes, slow growth may be an indication that our initial approach is not working, and we need to make adjustments to stay competitive and relevant. This could mean changing our product offering, targeting a different customer segment or exploring new sales channels.

By being open to change and willing to experiment, we can increase our chances of finding the right formula for success. I know from experience during the Blue Whale growth phase when we have committed to this plan, experiencing slow growth can be disheartening, but it shouldn't be the end for the whole plan. There are some strategic things we need to ask ourselves and adapt our plans accordingly.

Have we identified the correct target market for growth?

It is very possible that our past business experience and past target market has influenced the customer base that we are now targeting and this could explain why our current target market is not responding to our product or services as we expected.

There is absolutely nothing wrong with continually refocussing our approach as many times as we can to make sure we are reaching the right customers with the right messages to achieve growth.

During this Blue Whale process, we may need to expand our target market to reach a broader audience or narrow our focus to a more specific niche.

Task

Using the comparison customer data we have created throughout this whole process can we clearly identify if:

- Customer or consumer values have gone up – are they spending more?
- Have customer or consumer multiple purchase habits increased?

Diversify our offer to diversify our strategy

Another way to adapt our business strategy is to diversify our offerings. If we only offer one product or service, consider expanding our offerings to include complementary products or services. This can help you attract new customers and increase revenue from existing customers.

When we talk about diversifying our strategy we are talking about complementary products and services – ways we can add extra profitability – the old McDonalds trick of "would you like to go large with that?"

Focus on the marketing we are delivering to increase awareness of our business, our products or our services and re-evaluate using the data we are creating throughout this plan, is our marketing spend working and are we hitting the correct targets and outcomes needed.

Can we improve our customers experience by implementing new and highly targeted customer feedback surveys to identify areas for improvement, and likely incentives for those customers to participate? Consider moving into new markets much more rapidly than the initial plan allowed. Throughout the Blue Whale Plan we have talked about building growth on a regional, national and international basis, now might be the time to consider expanding our reach in a much more rapid way to help us attract new customers and increase revenue. This could involve opening new locations or selling our products or services online in brand new ways.

Slow growth linked to financial issues (it costs a lot of krill to feed a blue whale)

The financial health of our businesses during the Blue Whale process is a critical factor determining its growth trajectory and its speed. Often the slowing of growth or us not reaching those initial growth targets we set ourselves is due to financial challenges that we don't address or in some cases try to ignore. I know, I have been there, but ignoring these issues do not make them go away. To get our progress moving again and to speed up the growth, it is imperative to identify and tackle these financial issues effectively.

Cashflow management is a vital aspect of the Blue Whale growth process, inefficient cashflow management stops everything and most importantly gives a level of pressure and problem that every Blue Whale needs to avoid.

 Weekly task

We are going to identify if we are currently experiencing cashflow issues in our business and if these are hampering our progress. From the financial data we have, can you identify any of the following:

- Delays in receiving payments from clients.
- Unwarranted expenditure, that in hindsight you didn't think you needed to make – why?

> - Inefficient invoicing and collection processes – do we have invoices going out late? Do we have a backlog on collection?
> - How many of our invoices are over term?
> - Do we have shortfall in our cashflow because of insufficient capital or financing?

If you have identified issues in any of the tasked areas, this could be one of the reasons that our growth has slowed.

We are therefore going to implement some new financial functions to get a grip of this and to get the growth moving at the right rate and the right track as quickly as possible. Therefore, we are going to:

- Streamline our invoicing and collection processes, we are going to review, revise and implement some new and efficient invoicing systems and following up on all of our overdue payments on a daily basis to immediately improve cashflow.
- Review all of our expenses and identify areas where costs can be reduced will contribute to better cashflow management without affecting our customers experiences.
- Start to build an emergency fund for unexpected expenses or cash shortfalls to provide a financial cushion in challenging time and this is going to be no less than 10% of our total turnover.
- Set some new clear objectives that everyone in the organization buys into to help guide us to make qualified budgeting decisions and provide a framework for measuring progress.

Is slow growth happening because we are becoming too big too quickly?

The desire to grow and expand is inherent throughout the whole of the Blue Whale Plan and up until this point we have made an assumption that our rapid growth will translate into increased profitability and long-term success. However, sometimes slow growth may be an unexpected result of becoming too big too quickly and it is something to think about when developing and accessing our plans.

When we expand too quickly, some of the operational inefficiencies that we had as a slower growing business or a static business can become much more prominent. Things such as increased lead times, uncoordinated processes or communication breakdowns, that we had before but as a smaller business we were able to ignore or even navigate our way around become much more important and impactful.

As the business grows it becomes so much more challenging to maintain our streamlined processes, to keep our head in the data and keep this much larger beast on track and consequently, the business may begin to experience slower growth due to these operational bottlenecks.

We have covered the fact that this Blue Whale growth and expansion is putting a significant increase in overhead costs into play, such as the costs of additional facilities, personnel and resources and this in turn is putting a strain on the businesses overall financial health.

Has the Blue Whale process led to the hiring of numerous employees who may not share the same commitment or passion for our vision and has this dilution of company culture resulted in reduced employee motivation and engagement. This is one of the largest areas of slow or stalled growth but one that can be remedied and refocussed.

Communication is the key

The success of our Blue Whale Plan along every step of the growth journey relies heavily on the engagement and commitment of all of the partners, employees, suppliers and business associates.

Perhaps more than anyone, in order for us to get to our desired outcomes and reach our long-term personal and professional goals the biggest key to this across the board will be the communication techniques we employ to help foster a sense of ownership and purpose among team members.

By involving our whole business and all of the employees and others in the Blue Whale Plan and sharing the company's vision, to continue the growth focus we need to create an environment conducive to growth and success. But when the growth has slowed down, perhaps it's because our communication has become limited or even non-existent.

Have we, as Blue Whales, chosen to swim in a remote ocean now because it feels much more comfortable and we have engaged with the world at the start of this process and feel like we can go back to being the unnoticed largest mammal to have ever lived?

Transparent communication is vital in building trust and fostering a sense of unity, when team members feel informed and included in the decision-making process, they are more likely to support Blue Whale growth initiatives. So, to stop growth slowing and to make sure we bring everyone on our journey we need to revise and revisit and actively.

 **Task**

Clearly articulate the company's vision and long-term goals and explain how they relate to the growth strategy again and again and again. At least every six months.

Foster a culture that values open dialogue and feedback. Encourage employees to ask questions, express concerns and share ideas. This not only makes them feel heard but also helps in generating valuable insights that can aid in the growth process.

Make sure to give regular updates on company performance, no less than monthly, describe and illustrate our progress toward our goals and dispel rumours to ensure that employees receive accurate information.

As Blue Whales we know the importance of celebrating our own achievements but are we also celebrating the achievements, internally both big and small, by sharing stories of how our business has overcome challenges or reached significant milestones. This not only boosts morale but also demonstrates the tangible impact of employees' efforts alongside recognizing and acknowledging the hard work and dedication of individual team members. Sharing their stories explanations of how their contributions have played a crucial role in the company's growth.

Our intention to foster excellent communication skills throughout the business, helps everyone see the connection between the company's growth and their own professional development and is vital for the growth and development of the overarching Blue Whale Plan.

Feeling a loss of control as the biggest Blue Whale and the driver of the plan

As a Blue Whale business grows, it is absolutely normal for the business owner to experience a sense of loss of control, it is frustrating and hard and you want to cling on, but don't! The increased complexity and scale of operations now you are achieving what you have set out to achieve, means that you can no longer have the same level of input or oversight as before and this transition can be challenging, but it is essential to adapt to the new reality in order to facilitate continued growth and success. To stop growth stagnation and to really push things forward, you must adapt your role and change your emphasis.

Start to concentrate and recognize the skills and knowledge of our team members and assign responsibilities accordingly. Trust their abilities and give them the autonomy to make decisions and execute tasks, it's hard to do this but if they understand the company's vision, objectives and expectations through our enhanced communication as we just spoke about, we are providing them a clear framework to enable them to make informed decisions that align with the overall business strategy.

As Blue Whales we know, but we now need to acknowledge that change is an integral part of growth and we need to review it as an opportunity for learning and improvement. This will enable us to adapt more easily to the evolving demands of our business. As our business grows, so should our skills and knowledge.

Now is the time to continuously invest in our personal and professional development to stay ahead of industry trends and maintain our ability to lead effectively and most importantly enhance our journey to becoming an individual Blue Whale. So, we can see the overall importance of managing expectations and how it is critical when dealing with slow business growth, particularly in this Blue Whale process. But by setting realistic goals and timelines, staying positive and focussed, seeking support from a network of mentors and peers, and being open to pivoting or adapting our business strategy, we can overcome setbacks and continue to build a successful Blue Whale business.

It is important to remember that as a Blue Whale its size dictates that slow and steady progress is better than no progress at all, and that every setback is an opportunity to learn and grow. With determination, perseverance and a willingness to adapt, we will keep the Blue Whale Plan on track and reach those ambitions and goals.

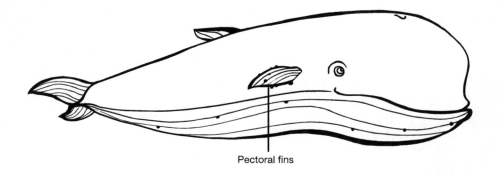

Pectoral fins

Chapter 11

The pectoral fins and innovation

The pectoral fins of a blue whale, the largest animal on Earth, offer a unique perspective when drawing parallels to innovation in business. Much like how the whale's fins provide stability, direction and balance, allowing it to navigate the vast oceans, innovation in business serves as a guiding force that steers organizations through the ever-changing market landscape.

As the Blue Whale relies on its pectoral fins to make precise movements, businesses depend on continuous innovation to adapt and thrive in competitive environments. By emulating the whale's agility, businesses can harness the power of innovation to maintain stability, adapt to emerging trends, and ultimately, achieve success in their respective industries.

Examples

Here are some examples that demonstrate the concept of Blue Whale businesses and provide various examples from different industries to help better understand their prevalence and significance. The businesses are likely to be large, influential and possibly dominant within their respective sectors.

By offering specific examples, I am aiming to demonstrate the diversity and scope of such enterprises, making it clear that their impact is widespread and pervasive, even if you may not be familiar with them. This helps to contextualize the concept, allowing you to appreciate the relevance of Blue Whale businesses in today's global economy. We will start with the biggest and the company you will probably know best.

Amazon

Amazon.com was founded in 1994 by Jeff Bezos, who was motivated by his "regret minimization framework" to participate in the emerging internet with his own start-up. Bezos left his job and moved to Seattle to develop a business plan for Amazon.com, which would become the world's largest online retailer.

After initially incorporating the company as Cadabra Inc., Bezos changed the name to Amazon.com, Inc. The name was chosen because Bezos wanted something exotic and different, and the Amazon River, the biggest river in the world, represented his vision of making Amazon. com the biggest bookstore in the world. Choosing a name that began with "A" was also strategic, as it would likely appear at the top of an alphabetized list. Bezos recognized the importance of building a strong brand and believed that brand names were even more important online than in the physical world.

Despite the potential for competitors to copy Amazon.com's model over time, Bezos was confident that the company's strong brand name would help it stand out and continue to grow.

In its early days, Amazon.com was operated out of the garage of Bezos's house on Northeast 28th Street in Washington and this was important.

Amazon's establishment, ambition and focus

Upon reading a report predicting an annual web commerce growth of 2,300%, Jeff Bezos created a list of 20 products that he believed could be marketed online. He then narrowed down the list to the five most promising products: computer hardware, computer software, videos, compact discs and books.

After careful consideration, Bezos decided to focus on selling books online due to the large global demand for literature, the low unit price of books, and the vast number of titles available in print. On July 16, 1995, Amazon.com officially opened its virtual doors as an online bookseller, offering the world's largest collection of books to anyone with internet access.

In just the first two months of operation, Amazon.com had already sold books to customers in all 50 US states and over 45 countries. Sales quickly soared to $20,000 per week, marking the beginning of Amazon's meteoric rise to become one of the world's most successful companies.

Where the Blue Whale comes in

As a successful online retailer of books, Amazon and Jeff Bezos could have continued to concentrate on this safe market. The market share was growing, turnover steadily increasing and over three years, expansion was happening at a global rate.

In common with all Blue Whales, Jeff Bezos had a desire for more, both personally and professionally. Going back to his origins and the data-based decisions he was making he was able to see other categories of goods that could be sold on a similar basis to books. Indeed, before books, Bezos had considered Amazon being an online marketplace for CDs.

Throughout the Blue Whale Plan, we have stressed the importance of data driven experience, of developing new markets and new opportunities based upon research and development and revisiting and re-interpreting everything we have done both personally and professionally to get to the place we have, before we started in the Blue Whale journey.

The Amazon story is a direct reflection of this, the ambition and focus of building a stable business that can then re-invent, adapt and concentrate on ambition and growth.

The Corning Story – A true Blue Whale

CORNING

Corning is a global technology company that has been around for more than 150 years. The company was founded in 1851 by Amory Houghton, a former Congressman, in the town of Corning, New York.

Importantly, in our Blue Whale Plan process, originally, Corning was a manufacturer of glass products including chimneys for oil lamps and glass tubing for scientific experiments, they made the glass for Thomas Edison's very first lightbulbs.

Over time, Corning expanded its product line to include items like railroad signal lenses and thermometers. In the 1930s, the company began to focus on glass research and development, which led to the creation of new products such as shatterproof automotive headlights and the first television tubes.

During the Second World War, Corning shifted its focus to support the war effort, producing items like glass radomes (radar domes) and lenses for periscopes. After the war, the company resumed its research and development efforts, resulting in the invention of a new type of glass called Corning Ware (Pyrex across the world), which became a household name in the 1950s.

In the 1960s, Corning made a breakthrough in fibre optic technology, which would become a cornerstone of the company's success in the following decades. In 1970, Corning invented a process for producing high-quality, low-loss optical fibre, which revolutionized telecommunications by allowing data to be transmitted at high speeds over long distances.

Throughout the 1980s and 1990s, Corning continued to develop and improve its fibre optic technology, expanding its product line to include optical amplifiers, connectors and other components. In 2000, Corning introduced Gorilla Glass, a durable and scratch-resistant type of glass used in the screens of many mobile devices.

Today, Corning is a global leader in specialty glass and ceramics, with products ranging from advanced optics and environmental technologies to laboratory products and life sciences. The company operates in more than 40 countries and employs over 50,000 people worldwide. Despite its long history, Corning remains committed to research and development, constantly pushing the boundaries of what's possible with glass and other materials.

Corning is a very interesting lesson, when you look at the Corning story the business has very large peaks and very large troughs in its history. In a Blue Whale context, Corning builds or invests something very successfully and in history has then created stability with this success, from which to leap frog and build further growth.

The business approach seems to be one of stability to allow risk and as such it has been able to navigate the icebergs of a changing world through the 19th, 20th and now 21st century.

The fins of Corning Blue Whale business must be very adept to spotting internal and external change and focussed on the larger ambition to have stayed on course over this sizeable time period.

Warburtons – a British institution

Warburtons is a British baking company that was founded in 1876 by Thomas Warburton in Bolton, England. Originally, the company produced bread and confectionery goods and delivered them to customers by horse and cart.

Over the years, the company continued to grow and expand its product range, eventually becoming one of the largest bakery brands in the UK. Today, Warburtons is known for its wide range of bread products, including sliced loaves, rolls and wraps.

The company is still owned and run by the Warburton family, with Jonathan Warburton serving as the current chairman. Under his leadership, the company has continued to innovate and grow, launching new products and expanding its reach across the UK.

One of Warburtons' most successful innovations was the creation of the Toastie loaf in 2007, which quickly became a best-seller in the UK market. The company has also expanded into the gluten-free market, offering a range of gluten-free bread products.

Despite facing challenges from changing consumer tastes and rising competition, Warburtons remains one of the most successful and well-respected bakery brands in the UK, with a reputation for quality and innovation that has been built up over more than a century of operation.

Warburtons is a story of not only Blue Whale business growth, but it also takes into account ownership, through managing family relationships and innovation in products to ensure consistent growth and development.

What do all Blue Whale businesses have in common?

My experience of working with Blue Whale businesses and whilst developing this Blue Whale Plan, all lead me to the same point as the three businesses we have highlighted, Amazon, Corning and Warburtons.

True Blue Whale businesses and leaders all share the same abilities across every industry today as it was in the 19th centaury for Corning that in an ever-changing business landscape, innovation plays the most crucial role in the growth and success of both the Blue Whale company and the Blue Whale business leader.

The businesses and leaders that prioritize and embrace innovation are not only more adaptable to change but also better positioned to maintain their competitive edge in the long run.

Innovation is the process of developing and implementing new ideas, products or processes to create value and drive growth. It is a crucial element for businesses that aim to thrive in a constantly evolving environment, but more importantly it opens the minds to the ideation process we spoke about, the businesses to pivot and change and perhaps crucially a group innovative focus on goal achievement.

As we can see from the examples as well as our own experiences in growing and developing our own businesses up until this point that businesses which can generate unique, ground-breaking ideas and implement them effectively are more likely to stand out in the marketplace.

The key to the whole Blue Whale process whilst developing innovative products or services is not only attract new customers but also to secure customer loyalty, leading to increased market share and profitability. By offering this innovation mindset and communicating the Blue Whale way of doing things, our businesses and us will naturally come up with new and improved products or services, we will and have attracted new customers and expand into new markets.

Importantly, personally and professionally, we will continue to foster a continuous flow of innovative offerings to help maintain customer interest and fosters brand loyalty, leading to long-term revenue growth.

We have seen, and we can see, through the three examples that to maintain our Blue Whale status over time that innovation is also essential in the re-invention of products and services.

As the world changes, as those icebergs flow and as the environment changes as the largest mammal that has ever lived, we must anticipate and respond to these ever-changing circumstances, our customers' needs, preferences and expectations and we must make sure that our Blue Whale businesses remain agile and adaptable to stay relevant.

This data-driven periodic re-invention and update to our products or services and indeed our markets and business, can help all Blue Whale businesses maintain customer interest and extend the lifecycle of their offerings.

By us using our newly developed data-driven approaches and adding new features, improving functionality or addressing customer pain points, we can keep all of our products or services fresh and compelling, as well as keeping our staff and stakeholders involved and focussed.

The intention of re-inventing products and services as seen in our Blue Whale examples, can open new markets and create additional revenue streams in markets that are complementary or develop as our business grows.

As we consistently use the data we are creating throughout the plan we are always targeting customer segments and addressing new pain points, this innovative approach is a way to dispel our reliance on a single source of income and ensure long-term financial stability, whilst we are on the Blue Whale growth path.

The Blue Whale Plan and longevity

We can see through both the examples illustrated in the plan and through those businesses we all know and love and would identify as Blue Whale businesses that the ability to innovate is closely linked to any Blue Whale businesses longevity.

Nurtured innovation both personally and professionally in a business environment results in a much higher likelihood of not just standing the test of time, but growing and thriving during that time also.

Blue Whale businesses and individuals that prioritize innovation are better equipped to adapt to changes in the market, technology and customer preferences, alongside – as the COVID-19 pandemic illustrated – resilient in the face of external threats, such as economic downturns or changes in regulations or indeed pandemics themselves. The ability of a Blue Whale business to pivot and explore new opportunities enables them to weather challenging periods and emerge stronger.

Blue Whale businesses by nature foster a culture of innovation and we are much more likely to attract and retain top talent on that basis. By focussing on our story and creating knowledge-based opportunities, creative, forward-thinking employees are drawn to organizations, such as ours, that value contributions and provide opportunities for growth and development both personally and professionally.

To ensure we reach our Blue Whale potential, everything we have researched and developed has led us to the knowledge that constant innovation is essential. Innovation enables us to stay ahead of our competitors by creating unique products, services or processes that meet our customer needs better.

The Blue Whale Plan innovation when communicated effectively to our employees and participants, enhances morale and fosters a culture of creativity and experimentation, leading to increased job satisfaction and retention.

By investing in the Blue Whale way of implementing innovation, personally and in our businesses, we can achieve greater efficiencies, better financial performance and create new opportunities for growth every day.

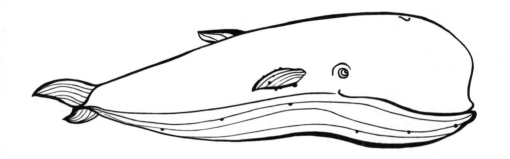

Chapter 12

The past to influence the future mindset of Blue Whales

Blue whales, the largest animals on Earth, nearly faced extinction primarily due to commercial whaling in the 20th century. Modern whaling techniques, coupled with a high demand for whale-derived products, led to the large-scale hunting of blue whales.

Whaling, the practice of hunting whales, has been part of human culture for centuries. However, the late 19th and early 20th centuries saw a surge in whaling activities, driven by the demand for whale oil and other by-products such as baleen. Whale oil was utilized in lamps, lubricants, and as an ingredient in soap, paint, and various other products. Baleen, a material found in the mouths of filter-feeding whales, was used to make items like corsets and brushes.

Advancements in technology further exacerbated the situation. The advent of steam-powered ships, explosive harpoons and factory ships enabled whalers to hunt and process whales on an unprecedented scale. These innovations made it easier for hunters to target and capture massive blue whales, leading to a rapid decline in their population.

During the peak of the whaling industry, there were few international regulations to protect whales from overhunting. Consequently, whaling continued unchecked, pushing the blue whale population to the brink of extinction.

Recognizing the dire situation, the International Whaling Commission (IWC) was formed in 1946 to regulate whaling activities and protect whale populations. In 1966, the IWC implemented a complete ban on blue whale hunting, which played a critical role in the species' recovery. Although blue whales remain endangered, their population has gradually increased since the ban. The IWC's efforts, along with national and international conservation initiatives, have been instrumental in preventing the extinction of these magnificent creatures.

From a Blue Whale Plan perspective, the rescue mission to avoid extinction and continue this growth process is now not about the business, we have all of the tools, strategies and knowledge to embark in the journey successfully. The rescue mission is all about us as Blue Whale business owners and our mindset and approach as we navigate this journey which at some points can be treacherous and difficult, and other times happy and joyful.

Building and growing your Blue Whale mindset can significantly improve your approach to life, making you more resilient, adaptable and open to learning, but how do we do this on a consistent basis, in a way that is manageable and perhaps most importantly in a way that delivers results.

The Blue Whale mindset

Acknowledge your mindset: Be honest with yourself about your current mindset, this is not a process of being hard or criticizing yourself, but rather a process of identifying when we have fixed-mindset thoughts and actively work to shift them back to our Blue Whale focus. There are a number of practical areas we can start to implement with immediate effect.

 Weekly task

Thought replacement

Over the next seven days really pay attention to your thoughts, particularly when you encounter challenges or setbacks. Stop and think is this a Blue Whale way of approaching this setback or challenge or have I fallen back into my old way of thinking about it.

Start to develop this as a habit of recognizing when you are having these retrospective approached thoughts.

Once you have started over the next seven days to notice when you have these thoughts, take a moment to pause and reflect on it. Acknowledge the thought without judgement, and remind yourself that it is just a thought, not a fact.

Now without judgement or fear, take the time to see a pattern and clearly identify the sort of fixed or retrospective thoughts you are having.

Now be specific is it things such as: "I'm not good at this", or "I'll never be able to do it".

The hard work starts here

Create a Blue Whale mindset statement that counters the retrospective mindset thought. Again, be specific, things such as: "I'm not good at this yet, but with effort and practice, I can improve", "I may not be able to do it now, but I can learn and grow over time". Repeat these Blue Whale mindset statements to yourself, either silently or aloud, and repeat it several times.

It is a fact that as humans, let alone Blue Whales that this repetition will help reinforce the new thought pattern and make it easier to recall in the future. Remind your mind that you are a Blue Whale and it really needs to get with the programme.

To keep up this re-training of your mind, to remind it, that you are no longer human but rather a Blue Whale, we are going to start practicing mindfulness meditation and journaling and build a six-month habit.

How to practice mindfulness meditation as a Blue Whale

We are going to aim as Blue Whales to practice mindfulness mediation three times a day for five minutes at a time. Morning, lunchtime and before bed. We are going to find a quiet and comfortable place where we can sit or lie down without being disturbed. You can use a meditation cushion or a chair to support your body if you are experienced at this. Now we are going to set a timer for five minutes each time we focus on this Blue Whale mediation and mindset release.

Close your eyes or lower your gaze to a soft focus, and take a few deep breaths to relax your body. Focus your attention on your breath, feeling the sensation of air flowing in and out of your nose or mouth. You can also focus on the rise and fall of your belly or chest as you breathe.

In your head, think about the size of the largest ocean you have ever seen. Not the waves crashing, rather the gentle ebb and flow and the calming waters during a warm summer month as you float lazily under the surface.

Whenever your mind wanders, gently bring your attention back to your breath and the sound of the ocean. Don't judge yourself for getting distracted or lost in thoughts – it's a natural part of the practice.

If you experience discomfort or tension in your body, notice it without judgement and try to relax those areas by consciously releasing the tension, repeat the word in your head, relax, relax, relax and be aware of the discomfort or tension and when it leaves.

When the five-minute timer goes off, slowly open your eyes and take a few deep breaths before returning to your daily activities.

This is a skill that requires regular practice to develop. Even if it feels challenging at first, stick with it and try to be patient and kind to yourself. Within a seven-day practice window you will start to feel different, your mind will be open and most importantly you will find yourself responding to things as you develop your Blue Whale business in brand new innovative ways.

Keep a record of the Blue Whale process and how it affects you on this journey

Write down your thoughts and feelings to track your mindset over time. Reflect on your journal entries to identify where the retrospective mindset patterns appear and work on shifting them.

Write down and repeat positive affirmations to counteract these thoughts. Things such as: "I can learn and grow", "Challenges help me become better". This will help to reinforce your positive Blue Whale approach and reframe your mind to mirror your Blue Whale mindset at all times.

Talk to yourself regularly

Develop a Blue Whale inner dialogue by practicing talking to yourself with a mindset, focussing on effort, persistence and learning. Encourage yourself to keep going and remind yourself that everyone has the potential to grow and improve. But make sure you are kind to yourself when you make mistakes or face setbacks.

All of us struggle, regardless of our mindset, our success or our journey, do not expect everything to be perfect – we know there are icebergs out there. Acknowledge that everyone struggles, and use any setbacks as opportunities to learn and grow.

Embrace these challenges as they present themselves and rather than avoiding them, seek them out. In a Blue Whale mindset, challenges provide opportunities to grow and learn, so see them as a positive part of our journey. Understand and acknowledge that failure is a natural part of the learning process, when we make a mistake as a Blue Whale, we analyse what went wrong and use that knowledge to improve.

Recognize the importance of hard work and persistence in achieving success. Praise your own efforts and those of others, rather than focussing solely on outcomes and understand that growth takes time and perseverance. Set realistic expectations and be patient with yourself as you work towards your goals.

Do not stop learning

This whole Blue Whale Plan and particularly this chapter is focussed on lifelong learning, cultivating your curiosity and keeping our minds open to new ideas, experiences and perspectives.

 **Task**

Develop a Blue Whale learning plan for yourself to help you to focus on gaining new skills and knowledge that can be applied not only to our businesses but also satiate our curiosity, this learning plan does not have to be only about business.

As a business owner, I love to learn about different approaches to business, growing my business and developing strategies, but I also love articles and podcasts on how to train my dog to do tricks, watching YouTube videos on how to convert a camper van and unfortunately for anyone who knows me, how to play every song ever written in four chords on the ukulele.

A learning plan should expand your Blue Whale mind.

How to create an effective plan

Identify your goals and needs and start by understanding what you want to achieve through your learning plan, try and be as specific as you can about the goals you want to achieve, areas where you feel you need improvement, and any specific skills you want to develop, I am always looking to start a ukulele orchestra.

Select the best learning resources for you, a learning plan isn't just about reading books, select learning resources that can help you achieve your objectives, things such as online courses, books, podcasts, conferences or workshops.

As a Blue Whale you know the power of data so develop some clear, measurable learning objectives that align with your goals and create a timeline that outlines when you will complete each learning objective. Stay curious and ask questions to learn more.

The Blue Whale magic of commitment

This whole Blue Whale Plan is designed for those that are looking for some level of magical transformation both in themselves and in their business. I know how this feels, I was the same. For 13 years I built a stable, interesting business, that I am very proud of, but it felt safe, predicable and somewhat boring. I had reached the point in both my personal and professional life where I needed more.

More personally for my own contentment and more professionally to reach the goals and targets I often envisaged I would be but hadn't really ever had a plan to reach them. The Blue Whale Plan was born out of this place. However, being a Blue Whale and having a Blue Whale business, requires courage, conviction but most of all it requires commitment to all aspects of the plan.

Whilst I think the Blue Whale Plan creates magical results, life may not offer such instant gratification and the power of the plan comes from staying committed to the Blue Whale goal. This journey is filled with challenges but also a myriad of opportunities for growth and self-discovery.

By staying dedicated to the Blue Whale Plan, you will experience life-changing moments that ultimately redefine your existence. I know, it works, I've experienced its power. However, commitment is the essential ingredient in pursuing the plan and realizing ours and our businesses full potential. It is the driving force that keeps us focussed, motivated and resilient in the face of the icebergs.

Making a steadfast commitment to the Blue Whale Plan, personally and professionally will empower you to overcome icebergs, learn from our failures and celebrate our successes. When we fully commit to this plan, we open ourselves up to a world of possibilities. This unwavering commitment will activate a magical transformation within you, enabling you to tap into the vast reservoir of your inner strength and determination. In doing so, you will begin to see the world through a new lens, viewing challenges as opportunities for growth and expansion and have a brand new perspective on life.

As we embark on this Blue Whale journey, we may face countless icebergs and obstacles, however, it is our commitment that enables us to persevere and keep moving forward.

Breaking down the plan into manageable chunks and following the data will enable us to celebrate each small victory along the way to strengthen our resolve, deepen our understanding of ourselves, and build our confidence in the vast oceans of the world. It will be in these moments, that we will catch a glimpse of the magic that commitment brings.

As we swim closer to our goals, we will notice subtle changes in our mindset and our approach to life, the once impossible will become achievable, and our fears will gradually dissipate.

If nothing else by following the Blue Whale Plan you will develop a renewed sense of self-belief and it will transform not only our personal lives but also the way we interact with the world around us. As you embrace your transformation into a Blue Whale your newfound confidence and capabilities, will inspire those around you to pursue their dreams as well. Our dedication to our goal will create a ripple effect on the ocean, motivating others to embark on their own transformative journeys.

This collective pursuit of dream and goals will elevate the energy of our community, our pod and will nurture a sense of togetherness across both our business and our life.

By supporting one another and celebrating our individual accomplishments, we contribute to a more connected and harmonious society.

The rescue of the Blue Whale is complete. Now go swim with freedom. Dive deep and have an adventure.

Summary

How to release yourself and your business into open waters

In the world of the Blue Whale Plan, having the right mindset can spell the difference between success and failure. This book has provided you with the tools and tactics necessary to foster growth and innovation in your business alongside delving into the mental shift that is paramount to becoming a Blue Whale.

The Blue Whale Plan is about setting ambitious goals, maintaining relentless focus and finding joy and excitement in the journey towards achieving these goals. It embodies the spirit of growth, adaptability and constant learning. It's the mindset and practice that can turn you and your business into a behemoth, just like the blue whale, the largest creature on Earth.

Staying focussed and motivated

I know myself as a business owner, you juggle multiple tasks at once. While this may seem overwhelming, the key to staying on top of things is focus. But focus isn't simply about working hard – it's about working smart. Concentrate your attention on activities that drive the most value for your business, activities that bring you closer to your goals.

Keeping your motivation high is equally essential. The Blue Whale Plan encourages you to find motivation in your vision, your purpose. Remember why you started this journey, and let this vision fuel your drive. It's not just about financial success but creating a lasting impact in your chosen field.

Setting and reaching your goals

Setting goals is the compass that directs this journey. However, goal setting isn't merely about setting any goal – it's about setting the right ones. As a Blue Whale remember to set ambitious yet realistic goals. Understand that growth and success are gradual processes, but do not be afraid to aim high.

Achieving these goals requires a systematic approach. Break down your long-term goals into smaller, manageable tasks. Set timelines, track your progress and celebrate small wins. These steps create a roadmap towards your ultimate goal and makes the journey less daunting.

Putting the Blue Whale Plan into action

Learning the principles laid out in the Blue Whale Plan is one thing but applying them to you and your business is quite another. It requires commitment, perseverance and a willingness to step out of your comfort zone. Don't be afraid to experiment with new strategies, to learn from your mistakes and to adjust your plans when necessary. Embrace change as an opportunity for growth. This flexibility and resilience are traits inherent in the Blue Whale Plan.

The joy and excitement of the journey

Adopting the Blue Whale Plan is not just about growing yourself or your business. It's also about enjoying the journey. Success is not solely defined by the end goal; it includes the learning, the challenges and the growth experienced along the way. Revel in the process of problem-solving, of overcoming obstacles of achieving milestones. Treat each day as an opportunity to learn something new, to improve to take one more step towards your goal. This is where you find the joy and excitement in using the Blue Whale Plan to make a difference to you and your business.

Remember: Becoming a Blue Whale both personally and in your business is not an overnight transformation. It's a continuous process of learning, adapting and growing. Adopting the Blue Whale Plan is the first step in this journey. It's about setting ambitious goals, maintaining focus, staying motivated and enjoying the process. As you embrace the Plan, remember to be patient with yourself and your business.

Change takes time. But rest assured, with the Blue Whale Plan and the strategies you've learned in it, you will be a ready to swim in an ocean that is so large it supports you and your business and the many others adopting this strategy with room for even more.

A Blue Whale may well be huge, but the space for you to operate will adapt and support you on every step of the journey.

Now get swimming.

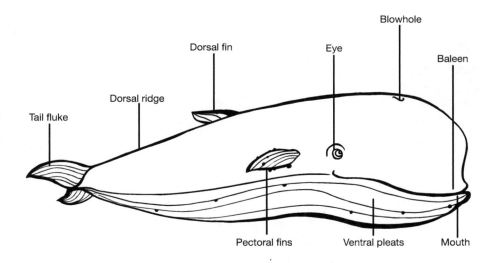

Dorsal fin   Eye   Blowhole

Dorsal ridge   Baleen

Tail fluke

Pectoral fins   Ventral pleats   Mouth

Acknowledgements

A **lison Jones:** Practical Inspiration Publishing, has been instrumental in making this book a reality, even when I thought my day job was just too demanding and I was not truly thinking like a Blue Whale, Alison and her amazing team, kept me on track with their enthusiasm and focus and she gave me an opportunity to meet other business authors and entertain them with my TikTok journey, which was so much fun.

Josie Dunne: I got to know Josie as an attendee of one of my workshops and she attended one of my programmes where we travelled to Boston to work in collaboration with Babson College. We then went into lockdown as the pandemic arrived. Josie has remained a true friend, encouraging and often threatening me to continue with my writing journey and the thing I am most grateful for is that she introduced me to the wonder that is Brendon Burchard and that has changed my life.

Cathy Rutherford: Cathy is one of my business partners and the person (other than my wife and family) that I could trust with anything. She is the most dependable friend and support and one of the kindest and compassionate people you will ever meet. She is also very shy and much happier behind the scenes, but she is the backbone of EMS.

Andrea Clarke: My other inimitable business partner. If you are ever in a bind, Andrea is the person you want on your side. She is focussed, determined and most importantly kind and compassionate. I think as business partners go, Andrea is also very patient and supportive and having me as a business partner means she has often needed to be patient. Andrea is also one of the bravest people I know and she's a real inspiration to me and everyone she meets.

The Babson 16: 16 business owners took a chance on me in 2020. It changed my life, changed the way I looked at business and has influenced everything I have done and said since. They just don't know what a difference they made to my ambition, but I will never forget it and will use it to power me further.

Every entrepreneur I have ever worked with: Every one of them in so many ways from so many backgrounds, so many life experiences have made a difference to me and my journey in supporting business owners through their lived experience. Positive and negative experiences have made me a much better business advisor, a better programme designer and teacher and most importantly a better person and I am very grateful to them all for trusting in me and my advice.

The author

Phil Teasdale is the Founder and CEO of Enterprise Made Simple Ltd (EMS) alongside being the Founder of a number of other businesses, including his most recent PhilTeasdale.com

He has built five seven-figure businesses personally and has worked with other 3,000 other small businesses on the same path.

Working alongside business Founders, Phil's skill is to combine mindset and business growth work to enable shifts in both perspective and ambition, using proven strategies, processes and systems.

Phil is not just researching this, but he is sharing his lived experience alongside his research and development, Phil himself and his business are two Blue Whales out in the wider ocean.

A particular commitment to female Founders and female led enterprises, Phil believes that for female returners to the workplace and those that have particular caring duties, the Blue Whale Plan and its implementation can really make a difference.

In 2010, Phil founded Enterprise Revolution CIC, a non-profit, focussed on increasing the life chances of females using business and enterprise as a conduit to opportunity in the Middlesbrough area – he is currently fundraising to create a grant and loan fund to offer small financial opportunities to those whose major barrier is low-level start-up capital and lack of support. Middlesbrough has the lowest level of female led businesses in the UK, the lowest level of females progressing into Higher Education in the UK and Middlesbrough is listed as a top three area of the UK as most deprived.

Phil lives and works in Middlesbrough, he employs from the local area and through his business Enterprise Made Simple Ltd, has directly invested over £500,000 in supporting an enterprise culture over the last four years.

Phil loves to deliver business content and has taken advantage of all media and social platforms to do this, you can and should actively link with, watch and follow the continuous content Phil develops on all platforms.

You can connect with Phil via social media, his websites or directly by email.

Social media

Linkedin: www.linkedin.com/in/philteasdale/
TikTok: PhilTeasdale.com
Twitter: @Teasdale
YouTube: @PhilTeasdale

Websites

www.philteasdale.com
www.enterprisemadesimple.co.uk

Email

phil@philteasdale.com
phil@enterprisemadesimple.co.uk

Index

A quick word from Practical Inspiration Publishing...

We hope you found this book both practical and inspiring – that's what we aim for with every book we publish.

We publish titles on topics ranging from leadership, entrepreneurship, HR and marketing to self-development and wellbeing.

Find details of all our books at: www.practicalinspiration.com

 Did you know...

We can offer discounts on bulk sales of all our titles – ideal if you want to use them for training purposes, corporate giveaways or simply because you feel these ideas deserve to be shared with your network.

We can even produce bespoke versions of our books, for example with your organization's logo and/or a tailored foreword.

To discuss further, contact us on info@practicalinspiration.com.

 Got an idea for a business book?

We may be able to help. Find out more about publishing in partnership with us at: bit.ly/PIpublishing.

Follow us on social media...

 @PIPTalking

@pip_talking

@practicalinspiration

@piptalking

Practical Inspiration Publishing

Printed in the USA
CPSIA information can be obtained
at www.ICGtesting.com
JSHW012016140824
68134JS00025B/2441

9 781788 603645